"Mike Cosper helps us make sense of w ... culture consumes, and he does it witho... the amount of TV and movies our cultu... ...., this book is a must read."

    Matt Chandler, Lead Pastor, The Village Church, Dallas, Texas; President, Acts 29 Church Planting Network

"Like Paul at the Areopagus, Mike Cosper walks through the cultural artifacts of our entertainment industry and effectively says, 'I can tell by your sitcoms and dramas and even your romantic comedies that you are a storytelling people who long for more. Let me introduce you to the Storyteller you don't even realize you long to know.' The result is a book that will change how you watch TV and movies. But more importantly, this might change the conversations you have with your neighbors."

    James K. A. Smith, Professor of Philosophy, Calvin College; author, *Imagining the Kingdom* and *How (Not) to Be Secular*

"Cultural engagement is a delicate but necessary balance for all who claim Christ. Mike Cosper insightfully examines narratives in pop culture to reveal the larger story of God at work in the human heart. This book is a must read for pastors and all those who seek to engage the culture with the powerful story of the gospel."

    Ed Stetzer, President, LifeWay Research; author, *Subversive Kingdom*; edstetzer.com

"Drawing upon a dazzling breadth of stories told through film, television, and literature, Mike Cosper examines—critically and charitably, wisely and generously—the culture-shaping power of stories and how all reflect in some way the grand story of creation, fall, and redemption. Skillfully and compellingly written, *The Stories We Tell* is essential reading for anyone consuming, engaging, or shaping the culture."

    Karen Swallow Prior, author, *Booked: Literature in the Soul of Me* and *Fierce Convictions: The Extraordinary Life of Hannah More—Poet, Reformer, Abolitionist*

"Mike has showed us the way of participating in culture and discerning where God is in it. It is easy to simply reject cultural creations in the name of purity. Or to receive them uncritically. *The Stories We Tell* will inspire a new generation of missionaries who seek to live in the world but not of it."

    Darrin Patrick, Lead Pastor, The Journey, St. Louis, Missouri; Vice President, Acts 29; Chaplain to the St. Louis Cardinals; author, *The Dude's Guide to Manhood*

"There is no one I would rather read on issues of popular culture than Mike Cosper. This book is not another 'here's how you find the gospel in Superman' project. Cosper analyzes popular culture with depth and with wisdom, seeing both the common grace of conscience all around us and the depths of human sin. As Cosper interacts with popular culture, he models for us how to listen to the voices around us in order that we might engage them with the mission of Christ. This book is about more than the media he analyzes. It is also a training ground for how to pay attention to our neighbors."

Russell D. Moore, President, The Ethics & Religious Liberty
Commission; author, *Tempted and Tried*

"The stories we tell rattle around in our minds, capture our imaginations, and give shape to our living as they echo the themes of God's grand redemptive story—creation, fall, and redemption. These are not only the themes of film, literature, and television, but are also the inescapable passages of every person's life. Cosper gives us new eyes to see and new ears to hear the stories we tell and in so doing invites us to celebrate our inclusion in the one story with a happy ending that actually never ever ends. I love this book and I think you will too."

Paul David Tripp, President, Paul Tripp Ministries; author,
What Did You Expect? Redeeming the Realities of Marriage

"Evangelicals are notorious for consuming mass quantities of pop culture behind closed doors and sanctimoniously railing against the culture in public. It's time to stop the hypocrisy and get serious about thinking theologically about the TV shows and films that stir our imaginations. In *The Stories We Tell*, Mike Cosper plays the role of the Interpreter in *The Pilgrim's Progress* by clarifying our favorite episodes and movies in light of both law and gospel, and urges us, 'Stay until I have showed thee a little more!'"

Gregory Alan Thornbury, President, The King's College; author,
Recovering Classic Evangelicalism

"Cosper presents a thoughtful, gospel-centered analysis of culture that will resonate with the current generation. Whether you love TV and movies or hate them, they are indeed the central sounds and images of our culture, and they call for discerning theological critique. And this book delivers. Mike Cosper tells us the story about the stories we tell, and does so wisely and well."

Grant Horner, Professor of Literature and Film, The Master's College;
author, *Meaning at the Movies*

THE STORIES WE TELL

CULTURAL RENEWAL

Edited by Timothy J. Keller and Collin Hansen

Joy for the World, Greg Forster

The Stories We Tell, Mike Cosper

THE STORIES WE TELL

How TV and Movies Long for and Echo the Truth

MIKE COSPER

Edited by Timothy J. Keller and Collin Hansen
Foreword by Timothy J. Keller

CROSSWAY

WHEATON, ILLINOIS

The Stories We Tell: How TV and Movies Long for and Echo the Truth

Copyright © 2014 by Mike Cosper

Published by Crossway
          1300 Crescent Street
          Wheaton, Illinois 60187

Cover design: Bryan Patrick Todd

First printing 2014

Printed in the United States of America

Unless otherwise indicated, Scripture quotations are from the ESV® Bible (*The Holy Bible, English Standard Version*®), copyright © 2001 by Crossway. 2011 Text Edition. Used by permission. All rights reserved.

Scripture references marked NIV are taken from The Holy Bible, New International Version®, NIV®. Copyright © 1973, 1978, 1984, 2011 by Biblica, Inc.™ Used by permission. All rights reserved worldwide.

Trade paperback ISBN: 978-1-4335-3708-0
ePub ISBN: 978-1-4335-3711-0
PDF ISBN: 978-1-4335-3709-7
Mobipocket ISBN: 978-1-4335-3710-3

Library of Congress Cataloging-in-Publication Data
Cosper, Mike, 1980–
   The stories we tell : how TV and movies long for and echo the truth / Mike Cosper ; edited by Timothy J. Keller and Collin Hansen ; foreword by Timothy J. Keller.
      pages cm. — (Cultural renewal)
   Includes index.
   ISBN 978-1-4335-3708-0 (tp)
   1. Storytelling—Religious aspects—Christianity.
2. Popular culture—Religious aspects—Christianity.
I. Title.
BT83.78.C67   2014
261.5'7—dc23   2014002412

Crossway is a publishing ministry of Good News Publishers.

VP		24	23	22	21	20	19	18	17	16	15	14
15	14	13	12	11	10	9	8	7	6	5	4	3	2	1

For my Dad: Thanks for buying the big TV.

And

For Sarah, who has endured my television addiction for all these years. Thanks for watching with me.

CONTENTS

FOREWORD

Timothy J. Keller

When I was a new Christian, I came across a book by Stuart Barton Babbage entitled *The Mark of Cain: Studies in Literature and Theology*. The thesis of the book was that human beings have an awareness of their own evil and sin—and of their need for forgiveness and grace. He ranged over the range of modern literature—from D. H. Lawrence's *Sons and Lovers* and *Lady Chatterley's Lover*, to Kafka's *The Trial*, George Bernard Shaw's *Major Barbara* and *St. Joan*, Faulkner's *Requiem for a Nun*, Steinbeck's *East of Eden*, Camus's *The Fall*, Hemingway's *For Whom the Bell Tolls*, and Sartre's *Nausea* and *No Exit*. He showed how these authors' stories and fiction bore witness to important aspects of the Bible's account of the human condition. In successive chapters he showed modern literature's witness to the inveteracy of evil, the impotence of the human will, the horror of alienation, the indelibility of guilt, the gift of pardon, the longing for immortality, the joy of grace, and the mystery of love. In short, he showed the fragments of the Christian story even in the stories told by the great artists of the modern era. Or, put another way, Babbage showed how the Christian master narrative made sense of all these other dark, gripping, and moving narratives.

Babbage's book had a profound influence on me. It was revolutionary for me to see how the biblical gospel's power was not confined to my inward transformation and life within the Christian community. It also helped me make sense of everything, even the works of literature written by often passionately anti-Christian authors. It helped me see that human beings may hold down the knowledge of God's reality (Rom. 1:18ff.), but in order to suppress and hold it down, they must actually possess it at some level. They know the truth, but they don't know it. And that is why parts of biblical truth can often be found—sometimes expressed beautifully and clearly—right alongside of the trivial or the false in the cultural products of the world.

Mike Cosper, like Babbage two generations ago, turns to the main storytellers of our time—but in the case of late modern culture, they are more often filmmakers than writers. Mike also rightly assumes that human beings cannot escape being in the image of God. He quotes postmodern writer David Foster Wallace saying, "We're absolutely dying to give ourselves away to *some*thing." Indeed we are, and in the cinema of our time, we also see the filmmakers bearing witness to the inveteracy of evil, the impotence of human nature, the need for pardon and love—and redemption. God will not leave himself without a witness, and he makes even the wrath of man to praise him (Ps. 76:10).

Mike's book will help readers learn to put the gospel on like a pair of glasses in order to see the good, the bad, and the ugly in our culture more clearly. This book will be especially helpful, I think, for Christians who preach, teach, and communicate the gospel. And, in the end, learning this discipline—of seeing God's story in the stories we tell today—will be a way for us to deepen our own understanding of and joy in the gospel we believe.

AN IMPORTANT WORD BEFORE WE BEGIN

This is a book about TV and movies. My goal here is to trace out the ways these stories intersect with the truth. I believe the Big Story of the Bible—creation, fall, redemption, and consummation—is so pervasive, so all-encompassing of our world, that we can't help but echo it (or movements within it) when we're telling other stories.

With that in mind, understand that I chose to discuss the particular stories in this book because they help make my point and/or I happen to like them.

Some are rated R. Some aren't, but should be. Some I found encouraging and redemptive. Some are downright devotional. Some I wouldn't recommend. Others I never want to see again.

I mention this up front because I want to be clear that the inclusion of a film or story is *not necessarily a commendation*. The issues about what we should and shouldn't watch are multilayered and complex. (See chap. 2 for more detailed discussion of this issue.) Use wisdom in exploring movies and TV shows that you're unfamiliar with.

I should also say that my tastes and preferences are eclectic, and this book contains references to content old, new, and occasionally obscure. You may not like anything I discuss here, and for that, I apologize. Who can account for individual taste—particularly the sometimes-low-brow taste of this author?

Similarly, you may have very different interpretations of the stories I explore. That's a good thing. Stories have a three-dimensional quality, and your perspective might be different than mine, enabling you to see angles I don't.

You also might think it ridiculous that I didn't mention your favorite show or film. You might think my examples could be better. I will say you're probably right, but I'm glad you've read enough of the book to discover my error.

Regardless, I will say this: the method I use to examine these particular stories and connect them to the bigger story is easily applied to different films, TV shows, and books, and you'll hopefully find something to take away with you.

Finally, and very importantly, *consider this your spoiler alert*. I discuss a lot of plots in this book, and will ruin the endings to most of them. You have been warned.

Introduction

A WORLD FULL OF STORIES

Kenneth: "Mr. Jordan, do you know why I love television so much?" Tracy Jordan: "Because despite cell phones, iPads, and computers, it's still the most effective portal for poltergeists?" Kenneth: "On TV shows, nothing ever really changes, the people you care about never leave, and the bad guy always gets what she deserves."

30 Rock, "My Whole Life Is Thunder"

Summer is a sacred time when you're a kid. The break from school feels like liberation, and even years later, we can look back with warm, hazy summer memories. Days spent on a sandlot or exploring creeks and woods. Family vacations, packed in a minivan, going to the beach or seeing Yellowstone, The Badlands, or Mount Rushmore.

My summer memories steer in a different direction entirely. The most vivid comes from 1992: the year we got the big TV. While my brother and sister were sweating away in brutal humidity at band camp, I was sitting in the comfort of air conditioning, two-fisting bowl after bowl of popcorn, watching hours and hours of television.

It was a perfect storm, really. My father had always been

kind of a technology hound, and for many years we'd had a La-serDisc player and surround sound.[1] Today, they are dinosaurs. That summer, the home theater went to a whole new level. We added both a forty-eight-inch rear-projection television (big at that time) and a satellite dish.

It was my job to accept delivery of the TV at our house. I remember a big box truck backing into our driveway and a pair of men moving the TV into our living room, unwrapping the layers of moving blankets and plastic wrap from its exterior while I signed for it, and leaving it to me to connect its various components to the rest of the home theater system.

I spent the whole summer under that TV's otherworldly glow. I was a well-established movie junkie by then, but the addition of the satellite stations opened unknown worlds to me. My parents had raised me on Hitchcock and *The Twilight Zone*, and in the coming weeks and months, the satellite would introduce me to Billy Wilder, Francis Ford Coppola, and Martin Scorsese.

I remember when I stumbled onto *Kafka*, an early Stephen Soderbergh film starring Jeremy Irons, and it blew my mind. Its dark surrealism was a gateway drug into the movies of Terry Gilliam and Sam Raimi—and if you wonder what the connection is between those three, watch *Kafka*—you'll see it.[2]

Even as I learned to appreciate the quirky corners of film-making, I never lost an appreciation for more mainstream stuff. A favorite saying of my parents was that "an ounce of pretension is worth a pound of manure"—a line taken from the über-chick-flick, *Steel Magnolias*. Elitism was forbidden in my house, so no matter how much I appreciated films by David Lynch and Quentin Tarantino, I was still able to appreciate the movies of John Hughes, Savage Steve Holland, and Nora Ephron. I can even appreciate a Michael Bay movie, so long as there are enough good one-liners and explosions.

It was a great time to be into television, too. I remember watching the pilot episodes of shows like *The X-Files*, *Friends*, and *Just Shoot Me*. NBC Thursday nights were still "Must See TV," and *Seinfeld* was the king of prime-time comedy.

For better or worse, this was my formative education. Don't get me wrong; I also read books (as I still do) and played guitar in rock bands, but those untold hours in front of that heavenly electronic glow filled my mind with a love of comedy, a love of movies and TV, and most of all, a love of stories.

Like most Americans, TV had me hooked.

ADDICTED TO TELEVISION

The profound and dangerous power of TV and movies is that they have ways of getting inside us, shaping the way we see the world by captivating our imaginations. And this explains much of the dissonance between what Christians think *about* TV and movies and what they actually watch.

Many Christians were raised to be suspicious of Hollywood entertainment, but all of the warnings seem to have done little to curb what people watch, except, perhaps, to add a patina of shame to any admission of viewing. (Think of the way people cringe when they admit they watch *The Bachelor* or *Real Housewives*.) We experience a cognitive dissonance—a conflict between what we think about TV and what we actually tune in to watch. Many of us hate the mindless entertainment of the "boob tube," but we watch anyway, confounding even ourselves.

Why?

I believe that dissonance exists largely because our behavior isn't primarily dependent upon what we *think* about entertainment, just as an addict's behavior isn't primarily connected to what he or she thinks about their addiction. As philosopher James K. A. Smith puts it, "Our action emerges from how we *imagine* the world. What we do is driven by who we are, by the kind of person we have become. And that shaping of our character is, to a great extent, the effect of stories that have captivated us, that have sunk into our bones—stories that 'picture' what we think life is about, what constitutes 'the good life.' We live *into* the stories we've absorbed; we become characters in the drama that has captivated us."[3]

 CHANNEL SURFING
Entertaining Ourselves to Death

Infinite Jest, a massive novel by David Foster Wallace (himself a voracious TV addict), asks a lot of questions about entertainment and addiction. The novel largely focuses on the Incandenza family. James Incandenza, the father of the family, was a brilliant and restless mind. He founded a tennis academy and became a film-maker. He also was a hopeless alcoholic.

A few years before the bulk of the novel's action, James made a film that is so spectacularly entertaining, it's lethal. Viewers insist on watching it over and over again, rendering themselves catatonic and losing the will to do anything else that keeps them alive. In the book, terrorists want to use the film to attack the United States, incapacitating its population.[4]

Throughout the book, Wallace explores the parallels between entertainment, addiction, and human nature. One character, a critic of our entertainment-addicted culture, says, "Your U.S.A. word for fanatic, 'fanatic,' do they teach you it comes from the Latin for 'temple'? It is meaning, literally, 'worshipper at the temple.' . . . Our attachments are our temple, what we worship, no? What we give ourselves to, what we invest with faith."[5]

In other words, our fanatical attachment to entertainment—our hours-a-day habit of watching sports or action films or *Project Runway*—is an expression of worship. "We're absolutely dying to give ourselves away to something," Wallace said in an interview. "If [*Infinite Jest* is] about anything, it's about the question of why am I watching so much [@#$%]. It's not about the [@#$%]; it's about me. Why am I doing it?"[6]

Infinite Jest challenges our mindless entertaining, asking us why the screen has a hook in us, and warning about the potentially dire consequences. Against the backdrop of addiction, Wallace shows characters who are deeply lonely, longing for human connection and struggling to find it in the modern world.

Storytelling—be it literature, theater, opera, film, or reality TV—doesn't aim at our rational mind, where cultural Christian convictions like "we shouldn't watch *Sex and the City*" exist. It aims at the imagination, a much more mysterious and sneaky part of us, ruled by love, desire, and hope. When people, against their better judgment, find themselves hooked on a show, we can trace the line back to find the hook in their imagination. And as Smith says, "When our imagination is hooked, *we're* hooked."[7]

"Stories seep into us," Smith says, "and stay there and haunt us—more than a report on the facts. A film like *Crash* gets hold of our hearts and minds and moves us in ways that textbooks on racism never could. This is because it is a medium that traffics in affective [emotional] images and such affective articulations are received by us on a wavelength, as it were, that is closer to the core of our being. Such compelling visions, over time, seep into and shape our desire and thus fuel dispositions toward them."[8]

The mistake is to think that we're rational enough to overcome the power of these images and stories. Consider, for example, advertising. Our inner rationalist knows that the cheap smell of Axe body spray is more likely to work as a sexual repellant than as an attractant, but the product sells because the advertising doesn't even attempt to be rational; it targets the imagination. The ads appeal to the hopes and desires of young men—namely, their own desirability—and the effect is more powerful than any rational appeal ever could be. *Wouldn't it be great*, says the ad, *if you could just spray this and find yourself wanted?* Such dreamy, wouldn't-it-be-great thoughts are at the heart of much of our marketing world, and they work because our imagination can take us into the world the advertisers promise, even if the products themselves cannot.

Our imaginations are like resident storytellers, playing images on the silver screen of our minds, and these visions are often hopelessly irrational. In fact, our fantasy worlds probably have more in common with an Axe commercial than with reality. Consider your own daydreams of lust, revenge, and success. They don't play out along rational lines, but are ruled by emotions—and are nonetheless powerful. That's why advertising works, and it's why we remain hooked to TV.

A show like *Keeping Up with the Kardashians* is successful, despite the general consensus that it's shallow and many of the characters are vain and unlikeable, because it connects with our emotional core. Our resident storyteller (our imagination) sees the glamour, wealth, and paraded sexuality through the lenses of hope and desire (women want to be the Kardashians, with their pampering, shopping, and sex appeal, and men want to sleep with them), and the inner rationalist—the voice in us that keeps bringing up how shallow, vain, and unlikeable the show is—gets confined grumpily to a chair in the back. He'll make a snarky comment or elicit an eye roll or two, but the storyteller keeps the remote control.

It's an uncomfortable tension, and it's not exclusive to Christians. Many people are quick to acknowledge embarrassment about TV consumption. In an episode of *Seinfeld*, Jerry Seinfeld wants to deny to his girlfriend that he watches *Melrose Place*, going so far as to take a polygraph test in order to maintain his denial. (He, of course, fails the test and she dumps him.)

Author David Foster Wallace, commenting on this phenomenon, said, "It's undeniable, nevertheless, that watching television is pleasurable, and it may seem odd that so much of the pleasure my generation takes from television lies in making fun of it."[9] We love to hate TV, even as we consume many hours of it. Like Seinfeld, many of us want to be thought of as people who don't watch TV. We know it isn't good for us, and TV itself doesn't pretend to be healthy, either. Instead, it recruits us into a kind of conspiracy of cynicism and irony, winking at us through the screen, even as it demands that we keep watching.

Consider how many TV shows are about TV shows (*The Newsroom*, *30 Rock*, and *Episodes*, to name a few), creating an *Inception*-like reality twist: we find ourselves watching a show within a show, giving us a sense that we're behind the scenes and in on a joke. We're not just another idiot in front of the boob tube: we've got a backstage seat, and with it, permission to laugh at TV's frivolousness.

30 Rock made the silliness of television a major theme. It's a sitcom about a sketch comedy show on a network owned by a multinational corporation and run by ruthless executives, and it mercilessly mocks them all. The sketches on *TGS* (the show that exists inside *30 Rock*) are eighth-grade humor (featuring fart machines and animal genitals), the stars are studies in Narcissistic Personality Disorder, and the main characters—Liz Lemon (Tina Fey) and Jack Donaghy (Alec Baldwin) are deeply unsatisfied with their lives. The whole thing could be seen as a sophisticated critique of television, if the show itself weren't everything it's mocking. *30 Rock* simultaneously mocks the immaturity of fart jokes while making fart jokes. It mocks the objectification of women while frequently objectifying their female characters.

TV shows often acknowledge that there are much better things to do than sit around watching TV. They present a world, as Wallace points out, that is much more exciting than a world in which we sit around watching hours of television, a world of beautiful and interesting people, playing out our cultural fantasies of heroism and justice in criminal dramas, belonging and friendship in sitcoms, varying themes of envy, judgment, and escape in reality TV, and love and lust in just about every genre. Wallace says,

> Since television must seek to attract viewers by offering a dreamy promise of escape from daily life, and since stats confirm that so grossly much of ordinary U.S. life is watching TV, TV's whispered promises must somehow undercut television-watching in theory ("Joe, Joe, there's a world where life is lively, where nobody spends six hours a day unwinding before a piece of furniture") while reinforcing television-watching in practice ("Joe, Joe, your best and only access to this world is TV").[10]

In the early 1990s, when Wallace wrote his essay, the average American watched TV for six hours a day. "Six hours a day is more time than most people (consciously) do any other one thing. How human beings who absorb such high doses understand themselves will naturally change, become vastly more spectatorial, self-conscious."[11] Today, those numbers have shifted down slightly, but only because we also spend much more time in front of computers, tablets, and smartphones. That time, too, is often spent being "spectatorial" and "self-conscious," busily broadcasting ourselves in social media and observing the lives of others.

A LOOK AHEAD

In what follows, I intend to explore our addiction to these stories. In particular, I want to look at their common threads, and I want to explore why we keep telling them, over and over again. I believe we're watching because TV and movies are both echoing and forming our desires, and I want to delve into what those desires really are.

I believe the gospel has given us a framework for the whole story of history. I want to explore the way our ordinary, everyday stories intersect with the bigger story that God is telling, and I want investigate what these stories reveal about being human, being fallen, and longing for redemption.

Chapters 1 and 2 will lay a foundation for the conversation, starting with an exploration of stories themselves in chapter 1, and looking at how Christians can engage with the storytelling world in chapter 2.

Chapters 3 and 4 will look at creation stories, first the idea of creation and paradise in chapter 3, and then the search for love in chapter 4.

Chapter 5 will look at fall stories, examining how storytellers wrestle with the fall and human brokenness. Chapter 6, "Frustration," will explore stories that illustrate the kind of fruitlessness and frustration we experience in a fallen world.

Chapter 7, "Shadows and Darkness," deals with our fear of

the unknown and our unspoken knowledge of darkness and evil, especially as we see it in horror and science fiction.

Chapter 8 looks at redemptive violence and how many of our stories anticipate bloody, sacrificial action to redeem humanity.

Chapter 9 looks at traditional heroes and messiahs, and chapter 10 looks at glorification—how our longing for fame is rooted in a much deeper, more ultimate longing.

Throughout this book, you'll find "Channel Surfing" sidebar discussions. These are brief moments where we change the channel and look at a different aspect of a given chapter's main idea.

THE GOAL OF THIS BOOK

It's important to know a few things before going forward. First, I'm not a film snob. I'm as happy to watch a Mel Brooks screwball comedy as I am a Terrence Malick film. I blame my upbringing, which taught me to appreciate even the cheesiest of comedies. I don't have a top-ten list of favorite film editors or cinematographers. I'm just someone who loves TV and movies, and who loves Jesus and thinks that these two passions aren't mutually exclusive.

I'm also not out to do any takedowns. After chapter 2, I won't focus much on the moral aspects of watching TV and movies. We can and should debate the issues that exist around violence, language, and sexuality in film, but that could easily take over this entire book if I let it. Here, I'm less interested in debating the merits of watching content than I am in understanding what drives it. I want to get to the heart of these stories. Why do we tell them? What motivates them?

I believe that the motivation for our stories is deeply connected with the gospel, and by thinking about that connection, we can more deeply appreciate both.

Finally, you should know that above all else, I'm a pastor who has had the joy of serving in a church full of creative people and movie buffs (and even a few film snobs). I'm primarily motivated to write for people like them. As I pastor, I grow most concerned over people who thoughtlessly consume media—be it literary classics or trash TV—and I include myself in that group. Our relationships to TV and movies have powerful, soul-shaping effects, and what we carry into our "dialogue" with TV and movies is just as important as what we take away. If we're thoughtfully engaged, our watching can be educational, edifying, and even a cause for worship.

Story is a great gift from a great storytelling God. There is much joy to be had in enjoying that gift as it pops up in the world around us. So with thankful hearts, let's begin to explore the stories we tell.

1

THE STORIES WE TELL

We live in the stories we tell ourselves.

Grant Morrison, *Supergods*

It's often said that we tell stories to know who we are—to understand ourselves and our place in the world. It's as though all of our stories are a way for the imagination to poke at the human condition, testing its borders and depths, looking for ways to understand the *why* behind the *what* of our lives. In his memoir, author Salman Rushdie describes how his father told him old folk tales and legends, teaching him that "man was the storytelling animal, the only creature on earth that told stories to understand what kind of creature it was."[1]

Stories help give us a sense of place. They stir our imaginations and help us to experience love, betrayal, hatred, and compassion that might be otherwise foreign. They prepare us for experiences like love, or help us process things like sorrow and suffering.

The way that we understand our lives, our relationships, our past and future is all tied up in story. Your past is not only a set of facts. It's also a story you tell. "I was born here, I grew up here, I married there, we had our children then, and we watched them grow up."

Your future, too, is a story, but it isn't built upon memory. It's a story of anticipation—hopes or fears that seem imminent and likely. "I'll go here, I'll do this, I'll try that."

Even your fantasy life, the daydreams into which you wander, is a story you tell. We drift off, playing out visions of winning the lottery, telling off our boss, fulfilling our loves or lusts, making things right with broken relationships, or escaping from the circumstances of the much less glamorous reality in which we live.

Stories both entertain and educate, occupying the mind and forming it at the same time. *Uncle Tom's Cabin* stirred the compassion of a populace, turning its conscience against the institution of slavery. It was also a gripping narrative, pulling the reader along in a story that one felt desperate to resolve.

Evolutionary theorists have tried to make sense of the brain's capacity for (and gravity toward) storytelling and fiction. Possessing a worldview that understands life through the lenses of natural selection and biological purpose, they wonder why so much human energy goes toward making up and retelling stories. Why imagination? Why fiction? Why daydreams and oral traditions? Why is so much biological energy dedicated to the storytelling organ in our heads?

Some theorize that we evolved a capacity to imagine in order to plan for feeding, hunting, and mating, and that once the capacity evolved, we started using imagination for stories as a side effect. Others theorize that storytelling is like the feathers of a peacock—something developed to help attract mates.

It seems to me that the answer is much more simple: we were made in the image of a storytelling God.

THE BIG STORY IN A WORLD OF STORIES

Christians believe an audacious fact. At the heart of our faith is the bold claim that in a world full of stories, with a world's worth of heroes, villains, comedies, tragedies, twists of fate, and surprise endings, there is really only one story. One grand narrative subsumes and encompasses all the other comings and goings of every creature—real or fictitious—on the earth. Theologians call it "redemption history"; my grandfather called it the "old, old story."

Jesus affirmed this one grand narrative in a moment of frustration with the Pharisees, bursting, "You search the Scriptures because you think that in them you have eternal life; and it is they that bear witness about me" (John 5:39). He wanted these men, whose lives were devoted to the Scriptures and to the narratives and history of the people of God, to see that it was all meant to point to him.

The apostle Paul got it, too. He stood in the courts of the pantheistic Romans, on their own sort of "holy ground" where ideas were exchanged and religions were compared, contrasted, and nitpicked. He heard their stories and their poetry, and he knew that ultimately the thing they were looking for was Jesus. "What therefore you worship as unknown, this I proclaim to you" (Acts 17:23).

We can see it, too. If the Bible is true, then it has a way of encompassing and overarching every story ever told. Our personal stories, our fiction, our literature, our television shows, and our movies are all accounted for in a sovereign God's design for the world. The stories we tell are all a part of the story he's telling. We tell stories because we're broken creatures hungering for redemption, and our storytelling is a glimmer of hope, a spark of eternity still simmering in our hearts (Eccles. 3:15).

The story told in the Bible encompasses past, present, and future. It tells a story that begins long before us and ends long after us, and it calls us to find our place in its pages. It shows God's people on a journey toward a wonderful and hope-filled climax. It shows God as the master storyteller—the writer/

director/star, if you will—rescuing Israel from Egypt and guiding them home to the Promised Land, weaving a surprising and gritty narrative that led from garden to wilderness, from Abraham to Moses to Joshua, from wandering to Promised Land to exile and back.

JESUS AND THE STORY OF GOD

God's story took a shocking turn when the King of the universe was born in a barn and walked among us. And God-in-Flesh didn't walk around dishing out moral advice and high-minded philosophical rhetoric; he told stories. Lots of them. People would ask him a theological or spiritual question, and Jesus's answer would begin, "Once upon a time, there was a shepherd," or, "There were seven brides . . ." As N. T. Wright once said of Jesus's ministry, "Stories change the world."[2]

After dying and rising again, Jesus commissioned an army of storytellers to carry on his mission. Look at the sermons in the book of Acts; they're stories. The entire New Testament was written by men who knew that they were living in the tension of a great story. Having witnessed the life of Jesus, they were now carriers of his story, knowing that it wasn't over. They knew that it would one day come to a rousing, glorious climax when he returned. Like the prophets before them, the apostles told a story whose ending had yet to be carried out, an ending foreshadowed with promises of final justice and restoration.

The Bible as a whole manages to simultaneously tell one big story and many smaller ones. Like Russian dolls, one can unpack them layer-by-layer. There's the whole narrative of redemption history, which contains the story of Israel, which contains the story of the exile and return, which contains the story of Joshua, Ruth, David, Hosea, and all the others. Each subsequent layer alludes to the whole, providing a new way of thinking about the whole. The story of Israel can be understood as a microcosm redemption history: it is a miniature of the whole. So can the exile. So can Esther. Within the Bible, stories shadow, reference, and echo one another. And Jesus gave us the key to uniting them: "they . . . bear witness about me" (John 5:39).

FINDING OUR PLACE IN THE STORY

The Bible also invites a kind of personalization and allegorization (like all stories do). Kids learn songs in Sunday school like "Dare to Be a Daniel," and preachers invite us to imagine ourselves in the shoes of Joseph, David, Paul, or Peter. Jesus told parables because he knew they were the way that we understand the world and our place in it. When telling the story of the prodigal son, he knew that we might see ourselves as the runaway prodigal, or the "obedient" and indignant older brother.

By identifying with these characters, we learn something about God, ourselves, the advancing kingdom, and the darkness around us. If we believe that the Bible is what it says it is—God's Word, perfectly crafted for revealing the truth and leading us to real, everlasting life—then we must believe there is something powerful and soul-shaping about stories. Why else would God use such a vehicle for revealing himself?

Not only that, we must believe that the story of the Bible— the story of salvation history—really is the greatest story ever told. It's the story that interprets and measures all other stories. It's been told in perfect order, in "the fullness of time" (Gal. 4:4; Eph. 1:10). It's a story that is both written into our DNA (Rom. 1:20) and impossible to believe apart from a miracle (1 Cor. 1:20–31). The world both longs to hear this story and hates its proclamation.

So what happens, then, in a world full of image-bearing storytellers who simultaneously long for redemption and hide from it? They tell other stories. Lots of them.

CHANNEL SURFING
The Romcom Gospel

There's no arguing with the fact that romantic comedies tend to have the same plots, but have you ever noticed that their form matches the form of the Big Story? Several years ago, I heard Martin Ban, pastor of Christ Church Santa Fe, refer to it as "The Gospel According to Chick Flicks."

Romantic comedies usually begin with some kind of "spark"—a romantic possibility between two people. This is followed by an original sin—a problem that stands between the two people ever getting together. The couple then has to find their way to redemption, and the movie ends with the two drifting off into the sunset, happy ever after.

Consider a few examples.

	You've Got Mail	Knocked Up	Notting Hill
Creation	Joe (Tom Hanks) and Kathleen (Meg Ryan) meet online.	Ben (Seth Rogen) and Alison (Katherine Heigl) have a one-night stand, she gets pregnant, and they decide to try to make a relationship work.	Will (Hugh Grant) meets Anna (Julia Roberts) when she comes to his bookstore. Shortly thereafter he spills orange juice on her. It's love at first sight.
Fall	Joe's mega bookstore opens in Kathleen's neighborhood, threatening her livelihood.	Ben's slackerisms are incompatible with Alison's career-minded life. They break up.	Anna's boyfriend shows up in her hotel room; Will appears to sell Anna out to the tabloids; Anna disses Will to her cast.

	You've Got Mail	Knocked Up	Notting Hill
Redemption	Joe discovers Kathleen's identity and works to make sure she gets to know him. He apologizes for putting her out of business. Kathleen apologizes for stereotyping Joe.	Ben puts his life together, prepares for a baby, and is there for Alison when she needs him.	Anna gives Will a Chagall painting. Spike (Rhys Ifans) tells Will he's "daft" for letting her go.
Consummation	Joe and Kathleen meet at the park, where she realizes that Joe is "Frank" from online. Happy ever after.	The couple comes back together in time for the birth of the child. Happy ever after.	Anna and Will get married and have babies. Happy ever after.

STORYTELLING IN THE IMAGE OF GOD

All human creativity is an echo of God's creativity. When God makes man, he forms him in the dirt, breathes life into him, and sends him out in the world (Genesis 2). We've been playing in the dirt ever since. Just as God took something he'd made, shaped it, breathed life and meaning into it, and transformed it into something new, so we set about our own business, taking creation, shaping it, and giving it new meaning and purpose. Clay becomes sculpture. Trees become houses. Sounds are arranged in time to become music. Oils, pigments, and canvas are arranged to become paintings. Various metals, glass, and petroleum products become iPhones.

The same is true of stories. There is nothing new under the sun, and our stories—no matter how fresh and new they might feel—are all a way of "playing in the dirt," wrestling with creation, reimagining it, working with it, and making it new. Our stories have a way of fitting into the bigger story of redemption that overshadows all of life and all of history. *Because that bigger story is the dirt box in which all the other stories play.*

The storyteller's raw material is the stuff of ordinary, everyday life: relationships, conflicts, love, loss, and suffering. Behind that raw material is the bigger picture of which we're participants. We live in a world that was meant for glory, but is now tragically broken. We hunger for redemption, and we seek it in a myriad of ways.

And so we tell stories that reveal the deep longing of the human heart for redemption from sin, for a life that's meaningful, for love that lasts. We tell stories about warriors overcoming impossible odds to save the world. Stories about how true love can make the soul feel complete. Stories about horrific, prowling villains carrying out a reign of terror, only to be vanquished by an unexpected hero. Stories about friendships that don't fall apart. Stories about marriages that last. Stories about life, death, and resurrection.

We tell other stories, too. The world is like a faded beauty who looks in the mirror remembering her youth, mourning the long-gone glory of Eden. She is now battered and scarred, not merely by age, but by tragedy, war, and defeat. She feels all too heavily how far she's fallen, and in her sadness she tells mournful tales of glory lost. Of heroes who fail and unravel. Of sin and consequences. Of evil that triumphs and prowls. Of darkness that swallows all who draw near.

TELLING THEM AGAIN AND AGAIN

Given any one of those plot lines, you could probably name a few movies and TV shows that fit. I'd be willing to guess that if you scanned through a list of movies playing at local theaters, you'd be able to accurately sketch the arc of each story. In truth, we don't actually go to the theaters (or watch TV) to be surprised. Occasionally it happens, but it's not the norm. The exceptions, like M. Night Shyamalan movies, prove the rule. Most of us were utterly shocked by the ending of *The Sixth Sense*, but by the time *Unbreakable* released, we knew what to expect from him. The "twist" at the end of *The Village* and *Signs* were part of what we expected when we entered the theater. We knew that Shyamalan was out to get us, and we both expected and enjoyed it.

But in most of the movie world, things follow predictable patterns. Princes usually rescue princesses, villains usually are defeated, love triumphs, evil is punished, vengeance is had, and so on. Meg Ryan and Tom Hanks made essentially the same movie three times: *Joe Versus the Volcano*, *Sleepless in Seattle*, and *You've Got Mail*. Each film followed a similar arc—a certain sense of tragedy and loss is healed when these two wandering souls find each other—but that didn't stop audiences from going to see the next one.

Characters like Batman, Superman, Spider-Man, and the Hulk have been rebooted many times, and though each has had hiccups along the way (I'm looking at you, *Batman & Robin*), generally speaking, the movies have all been worth watching. Why do we keep coming back? Are we too dumb to realize that the plotline of a Hanks/Ryan film is an echo of a movie we've already seen? Do we really think that this time, Lex Luthor might defeat Superman, or that Batman's inner demons might once and for all lead to his demise? Of course not. Something else is at work.

This pattern of repetition is even more noticeable on television. Shows like *The Mentalist*, *CSI*, *Castle*, and *Law & Order* all follow a predictable pattern. Crime is committed (usually in the first couple of minutes), the crime is investigated, leads run up empty, and suddenly, in the last five or ten minutes of the show, the real killer is revealed and the tension is resolved. Again, we should ask, why do we come back to the shows week after week? Do we expect that Patrick Jane (Simon Baker) might fail this week? Do we think that Richard Castle's (Nathan Fillion) "novelist's insight" is eventually going to run dry, and this week's crime will end up in the cold case files?

Some might argue that it isn't a given week's story line that keeps us coming back; it's the larger narrative, serialized throughout the show. So for *Castle*, it's the love story between Castle and Beckett (Stana Katic), and for *The Mentalist*, it's Jane's quest for vengeance against Red John. But again, these stories sound familiar. Do we think that Castle and Beckett will ultimately end the show happily ever after, or will their love story fail and leave them both broken and jaded? Many love stories in real life end just that way—why shouldn't our television shows reflect that? Likewise, do we think Jane will eventually catch Red John? Would it be more satisfying if Red John were to win, and the brutal murder of Jane's wife and daughter go unavenged?

Of course not. These broader narratives are—in the end—just as predictable as the shorter story lines. When a show ends on a note that doesn't satisfy the audience (like the legendary and intentionally unsatisfying ending to David Lynch's *Twin Peaks*), it goes down in infamy. People don't just tolerate stories that are repetitive—they crave them. "Tell me again," we say as we turn on the TV. "Will the bad guys lose this time?" we wonder, and we suspend our disbelief in order to go on whatever ride we're being taken on.

LOOKING FOR HOPE

It's the deep underlying insecurity of the fall that makes us crave these stories. On the one hand we want to understand why the world is the way it is. We watch tragedies and weep at the lostness and brokenness around us. We know that they're true. On the other hand, we watch movies with happy endings, and they stir a deep-seated hope in us—the same hope that made Sam Gamgee (Sean Astin) ask Gandalf (Ian McKellen) in *The Return of the King*, "Is everything sad going to come untrue?"[3]

The stories we tell over and over again—be it a romantic comedy, a Bond movie, or a horror film—ring with hope that the answer is yes.

It's this sense of longing and probing that we'll explore in the pages that follow. I want to be careful to say right off the bat that these stories *long for* and *echo* the truth; they don't always get it right. What they always do, though, is reveal something about the human heart. One who carves a log into an idol and cries out, "Deliver me, for you are my god!" (Isa. 44:17) has actually got it half right: he is in need of a Savior. He's got it half wrong too, and the silence of the wood should make that apparent—though too often, it doesn't.

This is a book about stories and how they reveal the heart's longing for the gospel. In particular, it looks at how this deep desire is evident in pop culture. It's common to argue that *The Odyssey* or *King Lear* reveals depths about the human heart; I happen to think the same can be said (though in different ways) about *Dexter* and *Here Comes Honey Boo Boo*.

The overarching story of redemption history—the old, old story—can be told through the framework of creation, fall, redemption, and consummation. God made the world, sin corrupted it, Jesus redeemed it, and one fine day, God will ultimately restore it. That's the story of the Bible, start to finish.

I believe that the stories we tell can be examined and understood in this light. The creative impulses of the human heart are always probing at these elements of redemption history because they are our story and they are our hope—even if it's the misguided hope of one writing a poem to an unknown god in Acts 17 or of one believing that a win on *American Idol* will satisfy his soul. Throughout the book, I'll use these movements of the old, old story—creation, fall, redemption, and consummation—to look at the ways we're telling our stories today.

It's important to say from the outset that I do not look at our stories as allegories or metaphors. Instead, I look at them as *evidence* of longing and desire. They intersect with, reflect, or parallel what the old story tells us about the whole of history. For instance, a fall story might not be a direct allegory or metaphor for what happened in Eden, but it certainly is trying to understand it, to wrestle with it.

I don't presume to know or speak for the intentions of the writers, directors, or actors at all. I simply believe that if art is accurately depicting human life, it will reflect both humanity's brokenness and the heart's longing for eternity, beauty, and redemption—all of which are found in the gospel.

As Christians living in the midst of these stories, we have an opportunity to both learn and bear witness. Stories teach us a lot about ourselves and our neighbors, and they provide windows into how our world is wrestling with the effects of the fall. They also present opportunities to respond with the truth. Just as Paul walked into the Areopagus and showed how a love song to Zeus was actually a cry out for the real, living God, we can look at the hope offered in the world's stories as signposts to the true Hero of history.

Before we dig into the stories themselves, we have to deal with one additional challenge. Whenever Christians talk about TV and movies, an inner conflict inevitably emerges: should Christians be watching them in the first place?

So before moving on with the discussion, we need to have a chat with the Church Lady.

2

HOW FAR IS TOO FAR?

> When you're young, you look at television and think,
> there's a conspiracy. The networks have conspired to
> dumb us down. But when you get a little older, you
> realize that's not true. The networks are in business to
> give people exactly what they want.
>
> Steve Jobs[1]

If you've ever worked in youth ministry, or attended one,
you can probably guess the most regularly asked question.
It doesn't matter what might have been discussed in a given
gathering, whether it was work or rest or salvation or the book
of Revelation. If there is an opportunity to ask questions, the
eager attendees will find a way to bring it around to the hot
topic of teenage Christian angst: How far is too far?

For most of those who ask, it's a permission-seeking question. It's a way to define borders so that the happy teenage
couple can skate as close as humanly possible to the edges.
Sometimes, working with youth feels like a perpetual cycle
of defining borders, encouraging kids to respect them, and
comforting those who transgress.

The same question emerges any time Christians (of any

age) wrestle with the borders between what's acceptable and unacceptable behavior. How much alcohol is too much? How much money is too much? How much attention to my image is too much?

TV and movies are no exception. Throughout my lifetime, I've observed a simmering level of hostility and suspicion between the church and the entertainment industry, lived out through boycotts, sermonic rants, and a point-by-point indictment of prime-time TV's lineup of shows posted on a central bulletin board of the church of my youth. Meanwhile, the entertainment industry strikes back with biting parody of Christians who take their faith seriously.

Sometimes (perhaps most of the time), the critics of entertainment have a point. TV can seem like a vast wasteland of exploitation, cheap laughs, trashy thrills, and glorified violence. The movies that thrive at the box office are often steeped in sexuality and graphic violence, and video games train young minds to kill, steal, and destroy. It's an ugly world.

But the question of "how far" (or "how much") still seems like the wrong question. It has its roots in one of two attitudes: that of the overanxious teenager and that of the Church Lady.

THE OVERANXIOUS TEENAGER

When you're young, you want to know how far you can go. You want to expand your horizons away from your family with later and later curfews, farther trips away from home, and the pursuit of ideas and identities that run counter to your parents'. "Teenage rebellion," as it is so often called, is as much about self-discovery as it is rebellion, but it can also carry a dangerous dose of sensuality and narcissism.

Some Christians adopt a similar attitude toward media. They probe the edges, wondering how far they can go, how much they can stretch the boundaries of acceptability. Is there a good Christian reason to read *50 Shades of Grey*? They'll find it.

I'm reminded of the Reverend Brown (Arsenio Hall) in *Coming to America*, who stands in front of a line of bikini-clad women in a painfully awkward scene, shouting, "When I look at these contestants, for the Miss Black Awareness Pageant, I feel good! I feel good because I know there's a God somewhere! There's a God somewhere! Turn around ladies for me please!" The ladies turn around, baring even more of themselves. Brown continues, "You know there's a God who sits on high and looks down low! Man cannot make it like this! Larry Flynt! Hugh Hefner! They can take a picture, but you can't make it! Only God above, the Hugh Hefner on high, can make it for ya!"[2]

Some attempts to find "redemptive themes" in culture are a lot like the Reverend Brown yelling and sweating in front of a group of overexposed girls and calling it creational theology. Piling Christian language and ideas on top of dehumanizing entertainment (like bikini contests) isn't a successful exercise in redeeming culture.

THE CHURCH LADY

At the other end of the spectrum is the Church Lady. Where the teenage mindset is motivated by the tantalizing thrill of sin, the Church Lady, like the Pharisees, is motivated by the tantalizing thrill of religion. The question "how far is too far" remains, but it is driven by self-righteousness. Defining borders allows you to know that you're safely within them, and (more importantly) it enables you to know who's outside of them. Borders are positioned to judge furiously and righteously.

Remember Dana Carvey's iconic Church Lady, who sees Satan creeping behind every cultural trend and fad? She represents the voice that's always keeping moral score, condemning Donald Duck for not wearing pants or accusing the Muppets of socialism on *Fox News*.

At the heart of the Church Lady is a cocktail of fear and pride. Fear drives those who worry that the world will spoil their good name or send their souls spiraling down to hell. Pride motivates just as well, because the goal of the Church Lady's life is always self-justification. You don't just want to be righteous for God's sake; you want to make sure you're a little more righteous than your neighbor.

Both the teenager and the Church Lady reasonably recognize that the world is a dangerous place, and that sin does indeed entangle, but both also misunderstand what it means to be meaningfully "in but not of the world." Both seek self-justification through behavior modification, one by skating close to the edge, the other by policing it.

The question itself is simply the wrong question. Those who ask, how far is too far?—whether at the movie theater or the youth group—have, in a way, shown their hand, revealing a heart that misunderstands what it means to be a Christian in the world. Our engagement should be motivated by neither the thrill of sin nor the thrill of religion, but by the thrill of the gospel.

So let's start with the gospel, and work our way back to entertainment.

THE GOSPEL AND CULTURE

The gospel is an announcement—it is good news—that God has welcomed us back into his kingdom through the life, death, resurrection, and ascension of his Son, not because we earned it or deserved it, but by means of his glorious grace.

That announcement, properly understood, provides guidance for living and being in the world.

The Gospel of the Kingdom

The kingdom that God invites us into is not something entirely new, but in large part the restoration of something old—the world as it was meant to be. Genesis 1 and 2 shows us creation in perfect harmony, a world of work, relationships, and worship, without any stain of sin. Genesis 3 shows how fast that world fell into darkness, and by Genesis 4, the world is a murderous and bitter place.

Jesus came and announced that the kingdom of God is here, a message that shocked and confused his followers, many of whom believed that he intended to overthrow the Roman government. But instead, he was announcing a restoration of a different kind of order and a different kind of King. God himself was reclaiming his world, all of which—every square inch—was his idea to begin with.

Jesus's announcement reminds us that every good thing— every good story, every talent, every act of beauty and creativity—is itself an echo of God's creativity. They are gifts God has given to his creation, small wonders that were intended for his glory in the first place and, indeed, reflect him in their own small way.

German astronomer Johannes Kepler once said that all of science was merely "thinking God's thoughts after him." The same can be said of the arts. Our ingenuity and creativity are merely an exploration of the ways God has prepared the world to display his own creativity. His gift of language held within it the possibility of poetry and storytelling. The resonances of wood, metal, gourds, and strings would lead to the discovery of music. The trees of the forest were designed so that one day we would discover guitars, violins, sculptures, and furniture hidden within them. Creation was built for playful discovery and invention by a God who is the Master of both.

In the light of the gospel, we can say with Jesus and with

saints throughout history that our world belongs to God. He is our King and Creator, and every time we encounter goodness and beauty, every time a story echoes a sense of justice or mercy or love or even wrath, we can say "amen," recognizing that the roots of all goodness go back to the God who made the world and filled it with his glory. The gospel of God's kingdom reclaims every good gift as the property of the Creator.

The Gospel of the Cross

Though we see God's good gifts all around us, we must be prepared to encounter the brokenness and twistedness that abounds as well. Stories of beauty and grace might also contain themes that are exploitative and dehumanizing with violence, greed, and sexuality. The world is fallen, and our creativity is often enlisted in ways that contribute to that fallenness, whether it's by crafting golden calves or skillfully lighting up a pornographic scene in a movie.

The story of the world took a dark and horrible turn with the advent of sin, and that turn necessitated the world's greatest tragedy: the murder of God's Son on the cross. The gospel of the cross tells us that through Jesus's life, death, and resurrection, we have been made right with God. It's both tragedy and triumph—a blessed disaster in which an innocent was killed to redeem a bunch of criminals and conquer death once and for all.

The cross reminds us that fallenness in the culture around us isn't something to be taken lightly. Sin is costly, and we can't smile and pretend not to notice it, or indulge it for cheap laughs and thrills.

It is here that the church ladies of the world hang their hats. The sinfulness of sin is plainly seen, and not just in the most extreme examples. Even our family-friendly prime-time entertainment seems at times to be skipping and whistling down the road to perdition, celebrating things that are harmful and destructive.

But the response to such content isn't as simple as the Church Lady would make it seem. A hedging, reactionary response seeks to avoid watching "sinful" content like the plague, and on the surface that doesn't sound crazy . . . until you start to think about the Bible. The criteria one might apply to media would cause us to censor our own Scriptures. If we hedge out sexual content, we lose the Song of Solomon. If we hedge out adultery and murder, say good-bye to King David's biography. Even the Gospels prominently feature sex, prostitution, paganism, demonology, political power plays, and public nudity.[3]

One of my favorite books of the Bible to examine in this light is Esther. It's a book about a Jewish girl who hides her identity and becomes a contestant in an ancient Persian precursor of *The Bachelor*. Esther sleeps with the king and makes quite an impression in bed, leading the king to make her his new wife. Meanwhile, a tangled array of plots emerges involving murder, conspiracy, and genocide. God's name isn't mentioned once in the book, and the only religious reference is a call to pray for Esther when she makes the decision to risk her life and plead for the threatened Jews before the king (a decision, some commentators note, that comes only after her uncle Mordecai blackmails her).

It's funny how often pastors and writers will reframe this story. They look for whatever tiny clues they can use to turn Esther into someone worthy of respect—a virtuous young girl who, because of her great character, was in the right place at the right time to save the day. But that's far from the case. Esther—in contrast to Daniel, who was conscripted into similar circumstances during the exile—was deeply flawed and compromised, and yet God used her to carry out his purposes.

CHANNEL SURFING
Christian Freedom and Food Porn

When thinking about what we should and shouldn't watch, we need to be consistent. We talk about "stumbling blocks" and "making one stumble" when considering sex and nudity, but do we apply that ethic to everything we watch?

For instance, "Move That Bus" (from *Extreme Makeover: Home Edition*) might have been the three most disturbing words ever heard on TV.[4] In the moments that would follow these words, the response from the crowd and the family can only be described as worship. People fall to their knees, hands in the air, in total ecstasy over the new house.

If we want to be consistent when evaluating TV shows and movies, we need to consider whether shows like *EMHE* or the programming on HGTV foster covetousness or idolatry of another sort.

Another example is food porn. This is not a term I made up; Anthony Bourdain has been using it for some time. Bourdain has had several "food porn" episodes on his series, *No Reservations*. He features gratuitous images of pork, cheese, chocolate, and decadently expensive foods.

Our appetite for food is very similar to our appetite for sex. They are both good things, when kept within God's great freedom-giving boundaries. But they can also become all-consuming and destructive to our health and well-being.

So we ought to ask ourselves, is the way we obsess over food on the Food Network a stumbling block? Does watching cooking shows cultivate a joyful appreciation of God's world? Or is something more sinister at work? Are we nurturing discontentment?

Food shows—like *No Reservations* or Bourdain's newer show, *Parts Unknown*—can be a celebration of creation, introducing us to the endless variety of tastes and places we might never otherwise see. But we should be cautious, realizing that our hearts are more sensitive and prone to wander than we might want to admit.

Few of the great figures in the Old Testament are worthy of much respect based upon their own virtues. From Genesis onward we see lies, drunkenness, sexual failures, prostitution, idolatry, and more. The impulse to whitewash these characters is misguided, based on a moralistic way of thinking about what it means to be a Christian. They were failures, messy men and women whose lives matter eternally because they inherited God's promises, not because they lived lives of unbending faithfulness. If we try to frame them all as moral heroes, we end up projecting that expectation onto ordinary Christians, and we lose an important core fact of the gospel: it's an announcement that frees sinners from the bondage of their failure and the tyranny of a standard they can never live up to.

This matters immensely when we think about the gospel and culture. We have only one perfect hero, and his story happens in the context of these other tragic, chaotic, and dark stories. The content of the stories we hear and tell can't be true without acknowledging—and sometimes delving deeply into—humanity's darkness. The Bible does this masterfully, and great stories explore this as well. In fact, far from making sin and evil off-limits in storytelling, the best storytellers go to great lengths to force us to stare it in the face, as Herman Melville did in *Moby-Dick*:

> The white whale swam before him [Ahab] as the mono-maniac incarnation of all those malicious agencies which some deep men feel eating in them, till they are left living on with half a heart and half a lung. That intangible malignity that has been from the beginning. . . . All that most maddens and torments, all that stirs up the lees of things; all truth with malice in it; all that cracks the sinews and cakes the brain; all the subtle demonisms of life and thought; all evil, to crazy Ahab were visibly personified, and made practically assailable in Moby-Dick. He piled upon the whale's white hump the sum of all the general rage and hate felt by his whole race from Adam down; and then as if his chest had been a mortar, he burst his hot heart's shell upon it.[5]

The timeless power of *Moby-Dick* is in its exploration of human darkness and wrath. Almost any good story is going to get its hands dirty in that kind of raw material.

We're not off the hook, though, from being discerning about what we watch. A few years ago I met with a church member who was struggling with sexual sin with his girl-friend as well as a porn habit. We talked through a variety of means for him to prevent and resist temptation—certain habits of prayer, adding content monitors to his computer, committing to less time online, moving the computer out of his bedroom, not taking his girlfriend to his apartment when no one was home—and he sincerely, earnestly made all of these commitments.

As the conversation was ending, he said, "Are you going to see such-and-such movie this weekend?" It was a gritty new film that featured gangsters, prostitutes, and strippers, and if the advertising was to be believed, would be sexually charged.

I searched for words for a moment, until, "Are you kidding me?" fell out of my mouth.

My friend seemed surprised at my response, and began to replay the question in his mind, wondering why I was frustrated.

"We've just spent an hour talking about ways to reshape your life so that you aren't in a place of sexual temptation, and you're going to see *that* movie?"

"Oh," he said, relieved. "It's fine, man. Movies don't affect me like that."

I shook my head. I had a genuine, but limited, sympathy for the guy. When you're addicted to porn, your threshold for stimulation gets more and more dramatic. Most porn addicts take a slow path toward stuff that's hard-core, and in comparison to his drug of choice this movie seemed downright tame.

What he failed to see—and what many of us fail to see—is that our consumption of media has cumulative, life-shaping effects.

Consider recent Neilsen surveys, which say that the average American consumes five hours of TV a day.[6] That's a lot. Probably the only thing we do more of is sleep. Maybe if you work a highly repetitive job, your task at work might be done more than five hours a day. For the rest of us, though, we're doing more TV watching than anything else.

If you do anything for five hours a day, it's going to have a transformative effect on who you are and how you see the world. Imagine that you switched to watching French programming. How would it change you? Certainly, through immersion in French language, you'd slowly pick up the language. But you'd also pick up other cues. For five hours a day, thirty-five hours a week, more than 1,800 hours a year, you'd be observing (and participating in) French culture. The way people greet one another, the way they share meals, their way of expressing affection and emotion, would bit by bit, in a subversive slow-drip kind of way, become part of your way of being in the world.

Think about all the ways that this is already happening. Most of us have a group of friends who feed on the same media we do, and the language, culture, fashion, and jokes from that world shape the way we live in ours. Inside jokes amongst friends are often littered with quotes and references to a canon of shared entertainment. No one ever decided it should be this way. This is simply the way media consumption affects us.

David Foster Wallace, in an essay from the 1990s, illustrated one example of this:

> When everybody we seek to identify with for six hours a day is pretty, it naturally becomes more important to us to be pretty, to be viewed as pretty. Because prettiness becomes a priority for us, the pretty people on TV become all the more attractive, a cycle which is obviously great for TV. But it's less great for us civilians, who tend to own mirrors, and who also tend not to be anywhere near as pretty as the TV-images we want to identify with. Not only does this cause some angst personally, but the angst increases because, nationally, everybody else is absorbing six-hour doses and identifying with pretty people and valuing prettiness more, too. This very personal anxiety about our prettiness has become a national phenomenon with national consequences. The whole U.S.A. gets different about things it values and fears. The boom in diet aids, health and fitness clubs, neighborhood tanning parlors, cosmetic surgery, anorexia, bulimia, steroid-use among boys, girls throwing acid at each other because one girl's hair looks more like Farrah Fawcett's than another . . . are these supposed to be unrelated to each other? to the apotheosis of prettiness in a televisual culture?[7]

To put Wallace's concept a little differently, we are habituated to watch beautiful people. Beautiful—as defined by our televisual culture—becomes normal, and a new pressure falls on the shoulders of everyone to live up to that impossible standard. It happens without any preconceived intentions, too. No one said, "We should turn America into a bunch of anxious, beauty- and youth-obsessed narcissists. Let's put beautiful people on TV and really jumble their brains!" Instead, because TV is a visual medium, it was natural to put beautiful people on display. Our hours-a-day habit turned that decision into something with culture-shaping power.

To go back to an earlier example, the friend I was counseling couldn't see the connections between his commonplace, everyday consumption of sexually charged movies and TV and his sexually charged life. He wanted to break the habit of looking at Internet porn and taking advantage of his girlfriend, but he didn't see how those habits were connected to his media habits, wherein he was regularly being trained to see women as objects and sexual gratification as something worth pursuing at all costs. Such training or formation happens on all kinds of levels. The stories of our culture—repeated regularly in various ways—are shaping our imaginations and desires. We think we're merely being entertained, but the power of story is being used to frame the way we think about love, marriage, sex, children, war, peace, nationalism, and more.

This brings us back around to the original question, which I think we can finally begin to address fairly. How far is too far? And for that matter, how much is too much?

In the light of the gospel, we can see that all that's good about TV and movies belongs to God (the gospel of the kingdom), and much of this book will look at the good. As suspicious as I am of television and movies, I believe there's a lot of good in them. The stories we are telling are indeed forming our hearts and minds, and not all of that formation is bad.

That said, the gospel also tells us that the world is a fallen place (the gospel of the cross), and the stories we tell are no exception to that rule. Enmeshed with the good is the bad. If we tell stories (as many argue) to know who we are, then our stories reveal that we are indeed creatures of glory and depravity. Our world desperately needs a Savior willing to sacrifice everything for us.

The Gospel of Grace

The third aspect of the gospel tells us that God saves us by his grace, not because we've earned it or deserved it. For a Christian living in the sinners-and-saints mess of a fallen world, I can think of no greater comfort.

It's the promise of grace that propels us out into the world without the fear of the Church Lady. While our stories are indeed shaping our hearts and imaginations, they cannot do any permanent damage to those who are in Christ. In other words, you're not going to watch a movie that will steal your soul; the world can't really hurt you. Instead, you can take comfort in knowing that you're forever secure in the hands of Jesus.

The last thing our knowledge of our security in Christ should do, though, is call us to some kind of indiscriminate license in our viewing. Shall we go on watching porn, so that grace might increase? As Paul would say, "Of course not! That's ridiculous! In the light of the gospel, nothing could sound more absurd" (see Rom. 6:1–2).

Grace shapes our encounters with the world by first promising that nothing will ever harm us eternally and second, by motivating us to better things, better standards, better ways of thinking about the things we encounter. Where the law motivates with the threat of punishment, grace motivates with the promise of joy. We can step into the world with a sense of invitation. This is our Father's world. What do we want to explore today? Grace enables us to see that the longed-for hope of some stories has its truer, better counterpart in the story of Jesus. By grace, we know we're sinners, and we can welcome the prophetic confrontations some stories offer for our hidden prejudices and assumptions.

Grace disarms the alarmist reactions of the Church Lady because it actually *expects* to find sin in the stories we hear. It disarms the teenager because it's motivated by the love of and for God, rather than an eagerness to be tantalized and thrilled by sex, violence, and the glamour of Hollywood.

It calls us, most of all, to a kind of thoughtful, mature engagement. We should think deeply about the media we consume because it will have a long-term effect on the way we look at the world. We should think about the way entertainment exploits real people—both trained actors and also the subjects of "reality television," turning their plights, struggles, and vices into cheap entertainment. We should think about the reasons we are laughing or crying, about the ways that our stories are promising redemption, salvation, and "the good life."

CONSCIENCE AND COMMUNITY

Thoughtful engagement with the media we consume requires two key ingredients, working together to answer our questions about "how far" and "how much": conscience and community.

Your conscience is your "inner voice," a voice that's shaped by your environment, your family, your convictions, and your habits. It's what Jiminy Cricket sang of to Pinocchio, encouraging him with the idea that generally, he knew better when he was going to do something wrong. For many of us, it's the voice that simply says, "Don't do it," right before we do something stupid.

We need to pay attention to our consciences, as they have a tendency to speak up just in time. If you're struggling with whether to watch something, ask yourself if you're struggling against a conscience that knows better. Paul warned Timothy about the danger of searing your conscience (1 Tim. 4:2), painting an image of one who burns his way over the objections of his conscience, scarring it beyond recognition with a layer of scabs and calluses.

Many of us likely have consciences that are already seared, or that have been malformed by a culture that is permissive and blind to the ways that sin has crept into our hearts. Because of that, the conscience *alone* isn't a good guide.

So beyond the conscience, we need community around us, friends who will speak up when they think our addiction to *Days of Our Lives* has become problematic. If you're watching something and all of your friends are shocked, that should set off internal alarm bells. Likewise, if you're anxious to hide that you're watching something, something is probably wrong.

Community can only protect you, though, under two conditions. First, you have to commit to be honest. If you're not telling the truth about what you're watching and how it's affecting you (e.g., I'm watching smut and I'm struggling with a porn addiction), community will do no good for you. Second, community is helpful only if your friends are willing to confront you—many friends are looking for a collusive partnership in indiscriminate viewing—and if you're willing to follow their counsel. If all your friends think your consumption of David Letterman is turning you into a jerk, and you aren't willing to give him up, then it's doing no good to ask for their input.

Together, conscience and community can go a long way to guarding your heart as you step into the theater or turn on your TV. This kind of thoughtful engagement requires us to make connections between our media consumption and our hearts. Cultivating a sensitivity to your conscience will lead you away from much trouble, and community will be there to guard you from blind spots and self-deception.

MISTAKES ALONG THE WAY

Living in the real world will lead you to struggles. Even if you throw aside the world of TV and movies, the stories they tell have a way of creeping up in other ways. We don't need a TV to fantasize about sex or revenge, to foster greed, or to nurture pride and judgment. In some ways, the sins that creep up when we watch media are as revelatory of character as they are formational. This is why it's good to know that over and above everything is the reigning comfort of grace.

Perhaps you'll find yourself dwelling on revenge fantasies or violent daydreams after a movie marathon. Grace abounds. Perhaps you'll decide that your boundaries around sexual content were too loose. Grace abounds. Seize the opportunity to learn from the experience, and don't repeat it.

Christians will draw up boundaries. Some consciences are more sensitive than others, and we need to make room in community for varying levels of maturity and comfort with our viewing habits. And to be clear, maturity might mean watching less TV, or it might mean freedom to watch more.

I confess that in the months that have passed since proposing this book, researching it, and actually beginning to write it, I've experienced a personal transformation in how I think about TV and movies. Author Harold Best once remarked to me that as he got older, he simultaneously became more convicted of his freedom in the gospel to engage culture, and his own sinfulness. The result was that while he believed in a great and wide freedom in Christ, he exercised his freedom in a far more limited way than he had when he was younger.

Researching this book has had a similar effect on me. Examining why we tell stories and thinking about the formative effect they have on our lives has caused me to be less enthusiastic about certain shows and movies, and more enthusiastic about others. I'm more sensitive to what I think is exploitive and dehumanizing, and less enamored with certain writers, directors, and actors.

What remains, though, is a love of stories and a love of the medium of TV and movies. It's an amazing gift we have today: from the comforts of our homes—or from nearly *anywhere* with the help of mobile devices—we can travel through time and space to the French Revolution, the war on terror, or a long time ago, in a galaxy far, far away.

But in fact, such an ability has always existed. God, in his wisdom, chose to give his image-bearers imagination, so that anytime we get together, we can sit down, tell a story, and be carried away.

3

THE GHOSTS OF EDEN

And the LORD God planted a garden in Eden, in the east, and there he put the man whom he had formed.

Genesis 2:8

The only true paradise is a paradise that we have lost.

Marcel Proust[1]

The history of our world is bookended by two visions of perfection: the glory of Eden and the hopes of the new heavens and the new earth. In the chaotic middle, where we now live, we are haunted by these visions. When suffering strikes, be it from a terrorist, disease, or the battles that rage within us, a powerful sense simmers within, telling us that this isn't the way the world was meant to be. We want suffering to end, but we also know that it never should have been here in the first place.

The paradise of Eden was how the world was meant to be. It wasn't merely a garden; it was holy ground, a sacred place where men and women were to live in harmony with God and creation. There, the whole experience of life was meant to be explored—work, food, sex, relationships, and rest—without any stain of sin or suffering. This was the life we were meant to live, and this is what we long for today.

Think about advertising for vacations. They promise an experience of paradise and perfection. Disney World ads present a joy-filled veneer, a land where families are all smiles, where worries melt away and dreams come true. Cruises and tropical destinations are presented in a similar light.

But of course, as anyone with young children at Disney World can tell you, reality is far from perfect. Children can throw tantrums and bicker there as regularly as they do anywhere, and married couples can have World War III in the hotel room of their tropical paradise as easily as they can at home.

Even though our experiences disappoint, our longing for Paradise endures. It haunts us because Eden was real. We sense its loss as we grope through trial-filled days, continually reminded of the imperfection around (and within) us. Because of this, our stories about Paradise and creation often include calamity and disaster. For instance, *Avatar*, *The Last Samurai*, and *Dances with Wolves* present us with idyllic, harmonious worlds that collapse when invaded by outsiders (humans in *Avatar*, white Europeans in *Samurai* and *Dances*).

These stories are like echoes and memories of Eden, where an intruder destroyed something pure and unspoiled. We're left lamenting a loss we don't fully understand. It's hard to articulate—something we feel in our bones and know most clearly when suffering strikes. We're like second-generation exiles who never knew the world they lost, but long for it nonetheless.

The creation story has left us suspicious of perfection, too, longing for its achievement but unable to believe it could actually exist. So when we visit the ideas of creation, paradise, and perfection in our stories, we see a variety of tragic tales.

Anytime we explore themes of perfection, starting again, and invention, we're dancing around Genesis 1–3.

These "creation stories" follow similar story arcs. There are paradise lost stories, where the ghosts of Eden hang over our visions of paradise and our longing for a more perfect world There are stories where humans play God, aiming for perfection, toying with god-like powers, and experiencing the disasters of their failure. These are also "flipping the fall" stories, where perfection and innocence is reinterpreted as something dangerous and naive, and like the Devil's own temptation of Eve, sin is presented as enlightenment.

PARADISE LOST

In what little we know about Eden, we can be certain that it was something glorious, and its glories haunt us still. Ever since the events of Genesis 3, we've hungered to return home. It's the impulse that sent explorers out to the ends of the earth. It's what Ponce de Leon looked for in Florida, what Cortez searched for among the Aztecs, and what sent Cheng Ho out from China into the Indian Ocean. It was promised to Israel as a land of milk and honey, and promised again to the church as the city of God. Paradise.

It's a resonant idea in pop culture. *Lost*'s island was like a character unto itself, haunting the castaways with a sense of mystery and hope. While on the island, many were desperate to escape and make their way back home, but once they got there, they realized their mistake. They were preoccupied with returning to the island, pained by the loss of a glory they didn't appreciate. "We have to go back," Jack (Matthew Fox) famously cried.[2]

We all want to go back. We want Paradise. That longing beckons every time we see a beautiful landscape or a hammock slung between palm trees.

CHANNEL SURFING
Texas Forever

Alongside the idea of Paradise is the idea of place. Ever since being cast away from Eden, humanity has had a restlessness, a sense of being adrift. We crave a sense of rootedness, of belonging.

Many storytellers have latched onto that sense and developed imaginary worlds that embody a sense of place. Port William, Kentucky, is the realm of Wendell Berry's imagination; it's a tight-knit community whose sense of place and connection is the treasure of his novels. As Burley Coulter says in "The Wild Birds," "The way we are, we are members of each other. All of us. Everything. The difference ain't in who is a member and who is not, but in who knows it and who don't."[3] A sense of belonging—what Berry calls "membership" —is a treasure and a gift.

A similar ethos runs through the TV series, *Friday Night Lights*. Set in Dillon, Texas, *FNL* tells the story of the community through the lens of high school football. The team's coach, Eric Taylor (Kyle Chandler), and his wife, Tami (Connie Britton), are the heart of the show for the first several seasons (and one of the best depictions of marriage on television), but as the show goes on, we see an interesting shift. The emotional center of the show moves away from the Taylors to Tim and Billy Riggins (Taylor Kitsch and Derek Phillips). When the series begins, Tim Riggins is a hard-drinking slacker, destined to go nowhere and accomplish nothing with his life. Over time, he develops a strong moral backbone, going to prison for his brother in order to spare him from being apart from his wife and child, and taking in a neighbor girl and looking out for her. While other characters drift away from the town, the Riggins stay put.

By the final season, Tim has come up with some money to buy a beautiful plot of land, and he begins to build a house there. In one of the show's last scenes, Tim and Billy are taking a break from building the frame of Tim's new house. Their sense of permanence is a solemn contrast to the transience of all the others. The Taylors have moved to Philadelphia. Others have joined the Army or moved to big cities elsewhere. But sitting in the hazy light of West Texas, it seems like the Riggins are in on a secret. West Texas is Paradise. They crack open beers, and toast, "Texas forever."

Such a vision is the backdrop for the movie *The Descendants*, a drama starring George Clooney. It's a gentle and beautiful story of tragedy, set amidst the dreamy backdrop of Hawaii.

The film opens with a Clooney voiceover: "My friends on the mainland think just because I live in Hawaii, I live in paradise. Like a permanent vacation. We're all just out here sipping Mai Tais, shaking our hips and catching waves. Are they insane? Do they think we're immune to suffering?"[4]

Clooney plays Matt King, a hard-working lawyer, husband, and father of two, whose wife Elizabeth (Patricia Hastie) suffers a traumatic brain injury after a boating accident. A doctor tells Matt that she'll never revive from the resulting coma, and a living will specifies that they can't keep her on life support indefinitely, leaving Matt to break the news to his children, family, and friends. He takes his youngest daughter, Scottie

(Amara Miller), to pick up his oldest daughter, Alex (Shailene Woodley), from a boarding school on a neighboring island, wrestling internally with how to break the news.

Alex is a classic troubled teen, with a history of bitter feuding with her mother and a taste for wild behavior. As the movie progresses, Matt tells Alex the bad news, and asks her to help him tell the others—Elizabeth's parents, their friends, and eventually, Scottie, her little sister.

As he breaks the news to Alex, the plot thickens. "Dad, she was cheating on you," she says. Alex had witnessed her mother with her lover, and when Alex confronted her, the war between them erupted.

Clooney and Woodley are both at the top of their game in the film, with heartbreaking performances as ordinary people in the midst of a terrible trauma. They find a kind of solace together, even as Alex brings her dumpy boyfriend Sid (Nick Krause), a spaced-out surfer kid, into the family's drama. He has a knack for saying the wrong thing at the wrong moment. Elizabeth's father eventually punches him in the face.

But Sid is more than just comic relief. As Matt wrestles with the opportunity to confront his wife's lover, he finds himself up late, with no one to talk to but Sid. Sid reveals that he recently lost his father in a drunk driving accident. Matt doesn't offer any great words of comfort; instead, he simply says, "Good night," and it's comfort enough. Their humanity shines through—in all of its beautiful brokenness. Like most of us, Matt and Sid don't need answers. They need the solace of community in the world that exists outside of Eden.

It's the juxtaposition of paradise and tragedy that makes *The Descendants* powerful. The beauty of the islands is otherworldly, something once pure and undefiled, now littered with tourist traps and resorts, broken homes and broken lives.

Parallel to Matt's own crisis is the journey of the King family. They're descendants of an indigenous Hawaiian princess, and the family owns land all over the islands, including a massive beachside acreage that is still undeveloped. Matt is one of the only descendants who remains wealthy, having never spent his inheritance, and is the only remaining trustee who has decision-making authority over the land that they all co-own. The others want him to sell the undeveloped property, knowing that they'll all stand to get a windfall of cash.

As Matt's family unravels, his reservations about the sale grow. Photos of his long-dead relatives hang like ghosts around his home, hearkening back to a misty and idyllic past—a paradise lost to the sprawling commerce of the island and the creeping shadow of betrayal, failure, and death. He never loved his wife well. He wasn't present with his children. He isn't what he thought he was.

The only place Matt sees hope is in the untouched purity of the land. The land of his fathers. The land of his youth. He refuses to sell, infuriating his relatives, but settling something in himself. It seems, perhaps, to be his attempt to stop the plaguing spread of suffering and death.

In one of the closing scenes of the film, Matt is in the hospital room with his wife when Julie Speer (Judy Greer), the wife of Elizabeth's lover, comes to the door. She knows about the affair, and she comes to offer her condolences and forgiveness to the dying woman who slept with her husband. It's a painful and awkward scene (brilliantly acted by Greer). The emotion is palpable as she offers forgiveness to the nearly lifeless body, alternatively weeping, wailing, and shouting through gritted teeth.

Confused and convoluted as all that emotion may be, Julie knows that the only thing that can heal the trauma to her family, to Matt's, and perhaps to all of us, is grace. It's cathartic for her, and catalytic to Matt, who only afterward can extend grace to Elizabeth himself, offering loving words to her dying frame and saying a heartfelt and pain-filled good-bye.

The Descendants is a rare and beautiful movie. The soundtrack—elegant and understated excerpts of Hawaiian slack-key guitar and traditional music—works with the backdrop of the islands to show how beauty and tragedy are held together in our gorgeous and broken world.

There is no paradise after Eden, no corner where the curse's cruel tentacles haven't spread. But in Christ, there is hope for such a place. In him, we can all go back.

FLIPPING THE FALL

Some would have us believe that going back to Paradise would be a mistake. While most of our stories that wrestle with the fall see it as a tragedy, occasionally other stories emerge that portray the fall as a necessary and even good thing. Garrison Keillor, one of our greatest American storytellers, refers to the fall as a "necessary sin," since "humankind [wasn't] meant to remain as children in the nursery Garden but meant by God to live real lives."[5]

These stories look at Paradise as a kind of trap, a naive and juvenile existence from which the Devil liberated us. Rather than seeing original sin as a bite from the poison apple, they see it as a Promethean leap, a step of boldness that left us scarred but wiser, stronger, and better equipped for the "real" world.

The Truman Show is a tale of heroic rebellion, rejecting "paradise" in Seahaven for the real world. Here, the creator— Christof (Ed Harris)—is a cruel manipulator who, by keeping Truman (Jim Carrey) locked up in the bubble, is keeping him insulated from the real world. As metaphor, Truman lives under the manipulative control of self-interested, malevolent masters, and his escape from naivety into reality is liberation, with hopes of real love and real life.

Imagine, though, what *Truman 2* might look like, where this celebrity who lived with the illusion of normality, simplicity, and purity is thrust into a world of paparazzi, stalkers, hideous crimes, and all of our fallen ugliness. We should wonder if Christof and the show's architects would appear as villainous in such a tale. Would Truman long for the days of peace and quiet in Seahaven?

Another example of flipping the fall is *Pleasantville*, a story of two teenage siblings. David (Tobey Maguire) is the nerdy brother who finds refuge in reruns of a cheery and idyllic 1950s sitcom called *Pleasantville*—a show in the mold of *Leave It to Beaver* and *The Andy Griffith Show*. Jennifer (Reese Witherspoon) is David's promiscuous and troublesome sister. Magically, David and Jennifer are transported into Pleasantville, a black-and-white paradise world with no crime, no heartache or suffering, and most clearly, no sex. David hopes to figure out a quick way back to the real world without tampering with Pleasantville, but Jennifer decides to make the most of it, introducing the town to sexuality by sleeping with the star of the basketball team. The day after their trip to lovers' lane, the team can't make a single basket, because each player has one thing on his mind: taking his girlfriend to lovers' lane.

Soon after, color begins to appear in Pleasantville, and the town divides. Colorization marks those who are awakened, and the primary means of awakening seems to be sex, though reading banned literature like *The Catcher in the Rye* seems to have the same effect. Sin is the discovery of something secret, unknown, and exciting.

Those who turn from black-and-white to Technicolor become the objects of scorn and suspicion, and the colorless persecute the colorful. The movie is rich with biblical imagery in the form of gardens, floods, and burning bushes.

The message is clear: though life in Technicolor isn't pain-free, it's better than life in black-and-white, which is pain-free but passionless. The imperfection of colorful life is a price worth paying in contrast to the naive and dull existence of cheery, wide-eyed innocence.

It's a creative, if twisted, response to Genesis 3, saying that life postfall is better than life prefall. We'd rather be free than pain-free, right? We'd rather have responsibility than blind obedience. We'd rather have art and pleasure and beauty—all inherently dangerous—than safe-for-the-family perfection.

But *Pleasantville* paints a deeply mistaken picture of Paradise. The pleasureless existence of Pleasantville is in no way a parallel to life in the garden.

In Pleasantville, a life without sexual shame is found only in a life of sexual repression. Sexual expression immediately results in Technicolor life—characters' "eyes are opened" and the world they see is suddenly more beautiful. The problem, says the film, is not sex, but the culture of fear surrounding it. It's a reversal of life in the garden. In Eden, human sexuality and sexual expression was mandated by God (Gen. 1:28) and celebrated in relationship (Gen. 2:23–25). The fall created the great barrier to all sexual intimacy—shame (Gen. 3:7). To see the fall any other way is to radically misunderstand the goodness of our Creator God and the glory of innocence.

Pleasantville and *The Truman Show* would have us believe that in the garden, the Creator was withholding some good thing from us. Only in rebellion can we find self-fulfillment. What such stories miss is that true fulfillment was available in the garden. God had given us everything—most of all, the presence of himself—and now the longing of our hearts to find happiness is simply a longing to go home.

The fall was a choice for less, not more.

The hunger for home seen in *The Descendants* is lost in *Pleasantville* and mocked in movies of the sort. That kind of hope is treated as idealistic and hopeless. Characters who long for utopia, or a simpler world, are laughable or worthy of scorn, like Cypher (Joe Pantoliano) in *The Matrix*, who wants to go back to a pain-free existence and is willing to be enslaved to the Matrix for it. Forget about the dream that was Paradise. This messed-up world is as good as it gets, so you'd better rid yourself of false rules and expectations and start enjoying yourself.

Stories like *Pleasantville* not only parody Paradise, turning it two-dimensional and shallow, but they also parody fallenness, pretending it's interesting and overwhelmingly good. It's smarter. Sexier. Imperfect, but better. *Pleasantville* can't deal with the real problems of evil, where the argument that "it's worth it" doesn't hold up. The same spirit of rebellion that leads to color in Pleasantville leads to genocide in Rwanda, fatherlessness in Chicago, and sex trafficking all over the world. *Pleasantville*'s capacity for dealing with the problem of evil is weak indeed in the light of real, heinous sin.

Reversing the fall in this way is like a child reacting to losing a toy as the result of misbehavior. "Well," she says. "I didn't really want it anyway." Pretending that the garden was a cage or a shallow existence might offer some self-important comforts, but it doesn't make the thought of the garden go away.

We wrestle with Eden, and even if our wrestling is an effort to reinterpret its very meaning, it reveals that deep down, it still haunts us. As Joni Mitchell put it:

We are golden
Caught in the devil's bargain
And we've got to get ourselves
back to the garden.[6]

PLAYING GOD

A third riff on the creation story combines elements of the first two. It recognizes—as the paradise lost story tells us—that an attempt at perfection failed. But like the stories that flip the fall, it also tries to tell us that the problem is with the Creator. In these stories, we see efforts at creation and efforts toward perfection, and the disastrous consequences that result.

Because we were made for a world that's perfect, the possibility of perfection lingers in the corners of our minds. We imagine cold fusion that gives us endless resources for energy, medicines that eradicate disease, political structures that bring peace and justice.

But of course, history shows us that none of these efforts has succeeded. And it shows us that we should not be terribly optimistic about our chances of achieving these absolute goals. Instead, technological progress is probably most noted as a shift in weapons technology—the Bronze Age, the Iron Age, the Space Age, etc.

As storytellers, we seem to have little tolerance for efforts at human perfection, or the hubris that accompanies them. Grasping at godlike powers usually ends disastrously. The Death Star was supposed to be invincible, until a Tatooine farm boy trusted his feelings and drilled two proton torpedoes down an unattended exhaust port. Perfect security systems like the CIA's in *Mission Impossible* or the personal security system in *Tower Heist* are foiled, as are plans for the perfect crime in movies like *Reservoir Dogs* and *Before the Devil Knows You're Dead*.

The story of the Titanic is another example, both as a historical fact and also in its many film versions (James Cameron's *Titanic*, or *A Night to Remember*, or my personal favorite, the *Futarama* episode, "A Flight to Remember"). The ship was billed as unsinkable, a monster of human achievement and engineering, and yet when it hit an iceberg, it sank with catastrophic consequences for those who had trusted in it.

Our most perfect creations—our efforts at playing God—always stumble into the inherent problem of human weakness, creation's unpredictability, and the impending threat of evil.

The consequences of playing God loom large in world history. We have brought a whole host of terrors into the world, many of which were created with good intentions. In 1867, Swedish inventor and industrialist Alfred Nobel developed dynamite, an explosive that made nitroglycerin more stable and therefore more easily applied to drilling, mining, and construction. Dynamite also turned out to be a powerful weapon, and in 1888 a French newspaper, thinking Nobel dead, prematurely published his obituary, calling him the "Merchant of Death . . . who became rich by finding ways to kill more people faster than ever before."[7] The murderous potential of his invention (and the legacy with which it saddled him) was haunting, leading Nobel to leave most of his inheritance to a foundation that promoted peace, science, medicine, and literature—the famous Nobel Prize.[8]

But the story of Nobel's dynamite is far from unique. The Wright brothers' airplane led to skies filled with terror at Pearl Harbor, and again in Manhattan on 9/11. By unlocking the power of the atom, scientists realized they could power cities, but that discovery left its hideous mark at Hiroshima and Nagasaki (not to mention Chernobyl and Fukushima). The train that united continents is also the train that shipped refugees to Nazi death camps, enabling that machinery of death to operate with terrible efficiency.

Playing God in *Frankenstein*

Our capacity for invention is matched only by our capacity for evil. Perhaps the most iconic creation story is *Franken-*

stein, first told by Mary Shelley and published in 1818, and retold and reinvented about a thousand ways since. In Shelley's novel, Dr. Victor Frankenstein endeavors to create life by reanimating the stitched-together parts of dead bodies and animals. Frankenstein is ambitious and arrogant, and he thinks little about the consequences of his success until the creature comes to life, fills him with terror, and sends the doctor running away, sick and disgusted. The creature then sets out on a murderous course of retribution, killing everyone Frankenstein loves as a punishment for bringing him into the world.

Shelley writes, "How dangerous is the acquirement of knowledge and how much happier that man is who believes his native town to be the world, than he who aspires to become greater than his nature will allow."[9] It is ultimately Dr. Frankenstein's pride, his willingness to meddle with things that are too great for him and to play God without counting the consequences, that lead to the murderous results of his creation. The moral, for Shelley, is that mere humanity is a good thing, something worth cherishing.

Her story is cautionary and seems almost prophetic, given the next two centuries of invention and ensuing disaster. "Man," cries her Dr. Frankenstein, "how ignorant art thou in thy pride of wisdom!"[10] He echoes Paul's words in Romans: "Claiming to be wise, they became fools" (Rom. 1:22).

Playing God in *Jurassic Park*

One thrilling twist on the "playing God story" is Steven Spielberg's and Michael Crichton's *Jurassic Park*. The movie begins with a sense of thrill and discovery. We learn that by extracting the blood of dinosaurs preserved in fossilized amber (through mosquitoes that have fed on said dinosaurs), scientists have been able to reconstruct "dino DNA." Jurassic Park, then, is a theme park where the world will be able to come and see these reborn beasts, alive and walking once again.

And while John Hammond (Richard Attenborough), the billionaire inventor of the park, wants us to believe that he's thought of everything, we can't help but feel a sense of foreboding right from the very beginning. Dr. Ian Malcolm (Jeff Goldblum), one of several scientists given a sneak peak of the park, tells Hammond, "John, the kind of control you're attempting simply is . . . it's not possible."[11] Like Dr. Frankenstein, there's an arrogance that surrounds the engineering of the park. "God help us," Malcolm says elsewhere. "We're in the hands of engineers."

In an almost cartoonish way, Malcolm is the voice of caution and reason, warning Hammond (and the audience) of the almost certain disaster that awaits them. "Gee, the lack of humility before nature that's being displayed here, uh . . . staggers me," he says, adding a little later, "Your scientists were so preoccupied with whether or not they could that they didn't stop to think if they should."

Hammond argues back, "I simply don't understand this Luddite attitude, especially from a scientist. I mean, how can we stand in the light of discovery and not act?"

Malcolm replies, "What's so great about discovery? It's a violent, penetrative act that scars what it explores. What you call discovery I call the rape of the natural world."[12]

Malcolm is supposed to be a "chaos" scientist, adhering to the chaos theory of unpredictability in complex systems. Chaos theory is often illustrated with the "butterfly effect": a butterfly flapping its wings on an African savannah can cause a ripple effect that ends with rain in Atlanta, Georgia. Within the story of Jurassic Park, Malcolm is constantly reminding the others that the consequences of their actions are unpredictable. They don't know what will happen as a result of their toying with nature. They've greatly overestimated their powers in a complex world. More than that, Malcolm is a voice of reason and humility in the face of such profound confidence in human ingenuity.

The story proves him correct. A greedy computer programmer at the park named Dennis Nedry shuts down the security system in an effort to steal several dinosaur embryos. The park descends into chaos as dinosaurs escape their pens and bloodshed begins. Nedry himself, along with many of the park's staff, are eaten by the resurrected beasts. Malcolm and a handful of others spend a long night and day being hunted by dinosaurs, barely escaping with their lives in the aftermath.

What we see is a common theme: we play god, inventing technology and creating abilities with extraordinary power. But the consequences of that are disastrous. This theme gets repeated again and again. We distrust ourselves as creators, having an awareness that the long-term consequences of our decisions are unpredictable. Jeff Bridges, commenting on *TRON: Legacy* (which explores similar themes), said, "I dig immediate gratification as much as anybody, but it happens so fast that if you make a decision like that, you can go far down the wrong track."[13]

That theme returns again and again, in *Tron*, *The Matrix*, the entire *Terminator* franchise, *2001: A Space Odyssey*, and other stories where our creations rebel against us.

Playing God in *Spider-Man*

Playing god can lead to personal destruction, too. *Dr. Jekyll and Mr. Hyde* is a story about man being destroyed by his own ambition. This theme shows up throughout the legacy of Spider-Man as well. In both the comics and the films, Spider-Man's villains often start off with good intentions. The Green

Goblin from Sam Raimi's *Spider-Man* was a government contractor named Norman Osborn who invented weapons technology with good intentions—protecting soldiers and keeping the peace. His suits of armor and flying surfboards were designed to give tactical advantage to soldiers and peacekeepers, as was a vapor that increases speed and stamina.

But when Osborn's contracts with the government look shaky and he fears losing them, he tests the vapor on himself. It overpowers his better nature, and he becomes a villain, a murderer, and a terrorist. The technology takes over, wielding fierce and terrible powers, spreading mayhem.

Similarly, Dr. Octopus, from *Spider-Man 2*, is a scientist with a utopian vision. He invents his mechanical tentacles to help control a fusion reaction that could solve the world's energy and environmental issues, but the experiment goes wrong; the tentacles become fused to his spine and overtake him. In 2012's *The Amazing Spider-Man* (which is a slightly different version of the Spider-Man myth), the story happens again. This time, the scientist experiments with DNA-splicing technology in an effort to cure disease and heal people who have catastrophic injuries. Once again, the technology overwhelms, the effort to make the world better is turned against the scientist, and he becomes the monstrous Lizard.

We could explore many interesting angles of the playing God theme in the Spider-Man stories. For one, I'm fascinated by how repetitious the series is. The stories basically share the same plot: a well-meaning scientist invents technology that corrupts him, turning him into a villain. Spider-Man, in contrast, was created by fate, accident, or Providence, depending on how you look at it. So while the human effort to play God and create something that makes the world better turns destructive and nightmarish, something else, something other than human willpower, creates the one hero who can stand in the gap between that destructive power and the rest of humanity.

Spider-Man as a comic book character was born in August 1962. America was in the middle of the space race, the Cold War, and the long, shadowy aftermath of World War II. The frightful power of the atom bomb hung over the whole world, looming with a perpetual threat of destruction. Like the powers of Spider-Man's villains, the power of the atom was discovered by well-meaning scientists, but was too seductive as a tool for power, dominance, and destruction to resist weaponizing it. We can debate all day long about the necessity of the bomb's use in World War II, but we can't deny that the existence of the bomb is evidence of a fallen world, where death reigns and humanity suffers.

The bomb gave us godlike powers, making us able to wipe out entire cities and, eventually, entire countries with the push of a button. The fate of the world, especially the world into which Spider-Man was born, seemed to be held in the hands of gray-haired men who wore suits, lived in shadows behind closed doors, and were unyieldingly committed to political ideology. The rest of the populace was caught in between these clenched and terrible forces. They built bomb shelters and practiced drills, hiding under their desks in schools while smart-aleck kids whispered, "They only do this to make us feel better."

Grant Morrison, a brilliant comic book writer and sort of philosopher of super heroes, described his own childhood in the shadow of the bomb:

> On television, images of pioneering astronauts vied with bleak scenes from Hiroshima and Vietnam: It was an all-or-nothing choice between the A-Bomb and the Spaceship. I had already picked sides, but the Cold War tension between Apocalypse and Utopia was becoming almost un-

bearable. And then the superheroes rained down across the Atlantic, in a dazzling prism-light of heraldic jumpsuits, bringing new ways to see and hear and think about everything.[14]

Spider-Man—the young Peter Parker—was a perfect hero to emerge in the midst of this Cold War tension. Almost any time we're introduced to Parker—in the comics or in the movies—he's a bullied outsider. A teenager. A bookworm. A nerd. An everyman, who happened to be in the right place at the right time to receive a spider bite that would empower him with gifts that could save the world.

We make weak gods, and our stories reveal that we're already aware of that fact. Our efforts at perfection and our stewardship of perfection result in disaster, and stories that seem far from religious show a grasp of a world where failure seems inevitable, and our hope for redemption hinges on a miracle—an outsider who will enter into the chaos and pull us back from the edge.

4

THE SEARCH FOR LOVE

Not many stories describe life before the fall. Only two chapters of the Bible describe that world, and the first (Genesis 1), though full of sweeping images of the created cosmos, is scant on particulars. The second (Genesis 2) offers only a few additional glimpses.

But our hunger for Paradise lost isn't the only story we can tell. Along with glimpses of that strange, harmonious world, we see another story. Examined closely, it's one that might surprise many of us, given the way we tend to think about perfection and Paradise.

> The LORD God took the man and put him in the garden of Eden to work it and keep it. . . .
>
> Then the LORD God said, "It is not good that the man should be alone; I will make him a helper fit for him." Now out of the ground the LORD God had formed every beast of the field and every bird of the heavens and brought them to the man to see what he would call them. And whatever the man called every living creature, that was its name. The man gave names to all livestock and to the birds of the heavens and to every beast of the field. But for Adam there was not found a helper fit for him. So the LORD God caused a deep sleep to fall upon the man, and while he slept took one of his ribs and closed up its place with flesh.

And the rib that the LORD God had taken from the man he made into a woman and brought her to the man. Then the man said,

> "This at last is bone of my bones
>   and flesh of my flesh;
> she shall be called Woman,
>   because she was taken out of Man."
>   (Gen. 2:15, 18–23)

Don't let familiarity with these verses cause you to breeze over them. Here is Paradise, a world without sin and decay. Everything is in perfect harmony and everything hums and buzzes with God's brilliant design. And yet *it is not good that the man should be alone.*

This isn't a moral statement; Adam wasn't evil because he was alone. Instead, it's an expression of incompleteness. God's creation is not done. It needs a bit more. Imagine that a painter brings you into his studio where a project is only half-complete. You see a canvas that is beautiful, but seems to need more attention. The image is roughed out, and the colors hint at what you know you're meant to see—a landscape, or perhaps a portrait—but it needs a few more layers. It needs the finishing touch.

In Genesis 2, God looks at man and knows that he's not quite finished. God could have created Eve to begin with; after all, he knew the end from the beginning. He also could have snapped his fingers and conjured Eve out of Eden's ether, but he doesn't. Instead, he goes through a journey with Adam, bringing each creature to him, searching for the helper the man longs for.

It's interesting to imagine this world without sin, where Adam feels dissatisfaction and where God himself acknowledges that it isn't good for him to be alone. We can see that even in a perfect world, we were made to be dependent, and that life is meant to be mutual and communal. God has surely made us so that we're supposed to be satisfied in him, and yet that satisfaction is made complete with the experience of love and community with other image-bearers. The world was good, but it wasn't good to be alone in it.

Here we should ask, why? Why *didn't* God simply snap his fingers? Why did Adam have to first endure a parade of cows, sheep, aardvarks, and wildebeests before he finally got to meet his wife?

I think the answer is this: the *story* mattered. It was better, for Adam, to go on a journey to find his bride.

By searching through the garden and cataloging every creature, Adam went through a sort of courtship with creation. He experienced a longing that went, for an unknown period of time (long enough, at least, to catalog the animals), unfulfilled. Ultimately, to meet the one he would love, he had to give something of himself. So God put him to sleep, took his rib, and made Eve.

When Adam sees Eve, he bursts out in response. The first song in the Bible is a love song, sung by Adam to his newfound bride. It's a moment that has been echoed a thousand times: when Etta James sang, "At last, my love has come along"[1]; when Romeo and Juliet first see one another; when *Sleeping Beauty*'s Princess Aurora and Prince Philip meet in the woods; and when, in *Arrested Development*, Buster Bluth (Tony Hale) sees Lucille 2 (Liza Minelli) from across the room without his glasses and falls immediately for "a brown area . . . with points!"[2]

Love at first sight. A transformative encounter where two people meet and are indelibly transformed.

Even in a world without sin, there are love stories, and love stories are always marked by longing, searching, and finding one another.

CHANNEL SURFING
A Beauty That Transforms

There's something redemptive about beauty. It goes beyond our ideas about the search for love or love at first sight. Russian novelist Fyodor Dostoyevsky famously wrote, "Beauty will save the world,"[3] and while few have slogged through the pages of *The Idiot*, from which the quote comes, many have resonated with his sentiment.

In the world of fairy tales, who can forget *Beauty and the Beast*, in which a prince is cursed so that his appearance matches his heart, transforming him into a hideous monster? Only when he encounters true beauty, and eventually true love, is he transformed.

Moonstruck reframes that story in Brooklyn, New York, where Loretta Castorini (Cher) gets engaged to Johnny Cammareri (Danny Aiello) and subsequently falls in love with Ronny Cammareri (Nicolas Cage), his angry, sullen brother who lost a hand in an accident and blames Johnny. Loretta falls in love with Ronny (she was never in love with Johnny), and Ronny is transformed. (There's a big comedy of errors at the end, and Johnny is happy about the whole thing, too.)

Yet another example—and one that's more earnest—is from Woody Allen's 1979 comedy *Manhattan*. The film features the self-involved lives of Isaac (Allen), Yale (Michael Murphy), and Mary (Diane Keaton). Each of these characters, and the others in their orbit, are career-minded and self-centered. Yale is cheating on his wife with Mary, and when he ends the affair, Isaac begins cheating on his seventeen-year-old girlfriend Tracy (Mariel Hemmingway) with Mary.

Isaac becomes infatuated with Mary, and he decides to break up with Tracy in hopes of a long-term, real relationship with Mary. In that moment, the film has a sudden moment of raw and honest emotion. Tracy breaks down weeping, unable to comprehend how casually Isaac has dealt in love and sex. By the film's end, Isaac realizes that he's made a huge mistake. He's lost real love and an authentic human connection with Tracy, whose innocence and sincerity is a stark contrast to the selfish connivances of the other characters. Isaac lies on a sofa reminiscing about things that make life worth living, and he remembers Tracy's face. He rushes to keep her from flying off to London for college, but he arrives too late. She's packed up and is prepared to leave. In their final moments, the roles are reversed, and now he earnestly wants her to stay, but she's grown cold. Just before the credits roll, she tries to comfort him, saying, "Not everybody gets corrupted. You have to have a little faith in people."[4] Here, they've both been transformed. Tracy's beauty and innocence broke through to Isaac, but tragically, his detachment and self-involvement has broken through to her, as well.

OUR SEARCH FOR LOVE

In our own lives, we tell similar stories of love and longing. It starts young, when little ones play house and tease one another. As we grow, the stakes grow more intense, as does the longing. Many of us can mark our lives with moments of deep regret over the way we've managed our own search for love and companionship.

And yet we continue to search for love, regardless of how

disastrous our previous attempts have been. In many ways, our journey is like Adam's: we search the world for the one our hearts long for, but find only disappointment. The search itself is a good thing, but in our fallen world, it's riddled with pitfalls and land mines.

I think it's because this longing for love and companionship is hard-wired into creation—it's part of the actual design of the world—that the emotions behind it have such power and sway over our lives. People do crazy, horrible, sad things in their search for love. They shipwreck their lives chasing fantasies and lying to themselves in hope that the right person will one day, finally and ultimately, make them happy.

And many of these stories are told nightly in prime time.

Have You Met Ted?

In 2005, TV viewers were introduced to Ted Mosby (Josh Radnor) on the show *How I Met Your Mother*. The show chronicles Ted's years of living in New York City after college, where he seeks to discover his own sense of identity, and where he seeks true love.

Ted's journey is accompanied by four friends: Robin (Cobie Smulders), Barney (Neil Patrick Harris), and the deeply-in-love couple, Marshall and Lily (Jason Segel and Alyson Hannigan). In season 1, Robin appears at first as a love interest for Ted, and throughout the show, they have a strange on-again, off-again romance that the audience knows will go nowhere. (Ted refers to her, in front of his kids, as "Aunt Robin.")

Ted is a hopeless romantic, and he desperately wants to find true love. The show keeps hinting that it's coming, but Ted gets discouraged again and again. He's left at the altar. He's dumped. He cheats on a girlfriend and ruins a relationship. He can't seem to find anything that is lasting, no matter how hard he searches.

The other cast members sit like angels and devils on Ted's shoulders. Marshall and Lily have been together since college, and their love is often what keeps Ted's hopes for true love, marriage, and family alive. Barney, on the other hand, is a cartoonish male chauvinist pig, who (at least for the first five seasons or so) serves to discourage Ted's search, appealing instead to a life of reckless debauchery and meaningless sex with as many women as possible. Ted oscillates between these influences, at times walking step-for-step with Barney, at times acting principled and certain that true love is out there.

The show reveals a lot about our culture's anxieties about love. Marshall and Lily's marriage is treated affectionately, demonstrating endurance through good times and bad, and arcing the story in such a way that the audience can't help but root for them, especially when their relationship is threatened.

Barney lives as the ultimate modern, bachelor, man-boy with a slick Manhattan apartment, a goofy obsession with laser tag, regular visits to strip clubs, and a rotating cast of sexual partners. A running gag on the show involves Barney's playbook—a catalog of the ways Barney deceives and beds women.

Barney is both celebrated and mocked on the show, as is the emptiness of his one-night stands. At times, Ted can't help but follow Barney down this trail, but he inevitably comes back to his senses, often exposing Barney's own deep insecurities in the process. We see, ultimately, that Barney's party-filled lifestyle is a veneer that hides a broken, distrustful soul, someone who was wounded as a child with the physical absence of his father and the emotional absence of his mother. His sexual conquests are an attempt to drown out his own deep sadness.

Ultimately, Barney is on the same quest as Ted, eagerly searching for true love, but unsure if it's possible. In an interesting twist, in season 8, Barney makes one final play from the playbook—this time, for Robin. He and Robin began dating in season 4 but broke up when she became convinced that they were bad for each other. But Barney wanted her back, cooking up an elaborate scheme to make Robin jealous. Ultimately, he engineered things so that she could watch him turn away from his male-bimbo ways, burn the actual playbook, and confess that she too still had feelings for him. They got engaged, closing the door on Robin and Ted forever, and ending Barney's sexual escapades in the show.

Ultimately, *How I Met Your Mother* affirms that we need more than sex. It's not good for man to be alone, and hooking up ultimately leaves people feeling alone.

But the show is also an affirmation of the goodness of the journey. Ted's journey isn't exemplary by any means, but his search, his longing, and his desire for a wife is a broken echo of Eden. It's truly not good for man to be alone.

Searching for Love at 30 Rock

In the introduction, we looked at how *30 Rock* mocks the uselessness of television. But another central theme of *30 Rock* is the search for love. In the show's first episode, Liz Lemon and Jack Donaghy are paired together in their workplace. Jack is Liz's new boss at NBC, where she runs a low-rated sketch comedy show.

Liz's cast and crew is a collection of insecure, immature, and dysfunctional lunatics, and Jack's tremendous ego is continually landing him in awkward situations with NBC, its parent companies, and the executives around him.

Liz is, for all intents and purposes, a successful New York career woman: climbing the ladder at NBC, living in Manhattan, and surrounded by the trappings of success. Jack, to an even greater extent, has all the makings of a modern success story: killing the competition, seducing women, and living the life of a thriving Manhattan socialite. His sexual conquests leave him feeling empty, though, and he's perpetually on the search for true love. Throughout the show, a parade of women move in and out of his life, and Jack is always looking out to see if one might be the next Mrs. Donaghy.

Liz's story is especially interesting in light of sexual politics and feminism. Throughout the show, she wrestles with why she isn't happy. Why hasn't the feminist dream revealed itself to be satisfying? She longs for a husband and she longs for children. These two desires lead her into a variety of absurd situations: returning again and again to a loser ex-boyfriend, pledging to marry someone she hates out of despair, walking out of the office with someone else's baby. For seven seasons, we never knew what might come next, but we all hoped that Liz would fall in love.

The show had a real heart. Where much comedy relies on harsh dialogue and cynicism, *30 Rock* showed us an earnest, sincere desire for love and family. It did so even as it skated the edge of harsh, cynical, and even perverse humor. Almost every character lived out a love story, including Jenna Maroney (Jane Krakowski), the raging narcissist who is the star on Liz's show. Drifting through a variety of meaningless relationships, she eventually fell in love and settled down (though when she did, it was with a cross-dressing man who performed as Jenna in an all-male stripper review). Even Tracy Jordan (Tracy Morgan), the deeply unstable star who figured prominently in the show, eventually had to admit that he loved his wife and wanted to remain with her—this in spite of his obsession with strip clubs and partying.

Reality and the Search for Love

No matter how bizarre a story gets, the basic ingredients don't change. We want to see someone search for and ultimately find love. Our interest is evident in our sitcoms and movies, and it's evident in the kinds of gossip we entertain, whether it's about our next-door neighbor or Taylor Swift. I think our obsession with gossip about love can explain two prominent phenomena in our culture today: tabloid journalism and reality TV. One of reality TV's truly breakthrough moments was a one-off show that revealed much about the search for love.

I have vivid memories of a night in January of 2000, flipping channels with my wife and landing on what would become an infamous program on FOX. It was a reality show about the search for love called *Who Wants to Marry a Multi-Millionaire?*

The show aired to an audience of twenty-two million people, who collectively watched with mouths agape like passersby at a traffic pileup. Twenty-two million people, collectively wondering if the world would come to an end at any moment. Women from all fifty states paraded across a Las Vegas stage, answering questions in what was half beauty pageant and half game show, while a millionaire bachelor stood silhouetted behind a screen.

The dubiously named "prize" went to Darva Conger, who before our very eyes became the poster child for bad decisions. Millionaire Rick Rockwell appeared from behind the screen to meet his bride, and the two immediately exchanged vows, with Rockwell planting a big, forced kiss on Conger just before credits rolled.

There's a scene in *Gladiator* where Maximus (Russell Crowe) walks into an arena with a half dozen warriors awaiting him. He quickly eviscerates them—too quickly for the crowd's pleasure—ending the show by severing the head of his final opponent. "Are you not entertained?" he yells at the crowd as he walks amongst the strewn body parts and carnage. "Are you not entertained?"[5]

Somewhere in the world, while balloons and streamers fell

over that Las Vegas audience and Darva Conger learned the meaning of the word *regret*, TV executives with wild eyes, standing before the fearsome glow of their televisions, yelled, "Are you not entertained?"

Perhaps the most tragic moment of the whole thing came moments before Conger won, when the two final contestants were interviewed. One of the two—I can't recall which one— broke the facade of fun and adventure for a moment. The show's host asked the contestants why they were there—what were they searching for? With a hint of a tremble in her voice, one of the women said that she'd been searching for love her whole life, and in the end had come up wanting. Who's to say this wasn't a chance at the real thing—the real magic of love and destiny? It was a sad and human moment in the midst of carnival-like chaos.

The show struck a nerve for many reasons. On the one hand, as the contestant's comments remind us, there's at least a shadow of a real-life fairy tale. Someone ordinary could marry a "prince" and wake up in love and rich and happy. On the other hand, the show was revolting. The audience was bewildered at the exploitation of the girls (what kind of person signs up for this?), the millionaire (what kind of man searches for a wife like this?), and themselves as they stood transfixed. Fairy tales usually involve love at first sight, not a near-arbitrary (at best) or utterly vacuous (more likely) process of elimination.

What that show ultimately revealed—and what the last twenty years of reality programming have proven—is that for reality stars, the story is never over. Overnight, Darva and Rick became celebrities and the subject of scrutiny from tabloid media. Millionaire Rick Rockwell was soon exposed as an *almost* millionaire, with disputable accumulated wealth, a fake last name, and a restraining order for domestic violence. Conger, it seems, loathed him immediately, making sure the world knew that they never consummated their vows. She filed for an annulment within days of returning from their "honeymoon" and spent the next year or so experiencing the odd tension that has been the standard experience of many reality stars—the tension between enjoying (exploiting) their celebrity, and wanting to be left alone.

At one point Conger said, "You know, I really liked my life and I still do want to get out of the public eye. I don't want to be making the rounds of the talk shows." Ironically, she made these comments while on *The Today Show*, promoting her nude pictorial in *Playboy*. You can't make this stuff up, folks.

Right there—in the tension between being "normal" and being famous, between being a self-proclaimed "good Christian girl" as Conger claimed to be and being a *Playboy* girl-of-the-month—is the hypnotic power of reality television and tabloid journalism. Just as the world watched entranced as she won her contest, they watched entranced as she became a living contradiction. Having experienced the intoxicating effects of stardom and "easy" money, she willingly gave up greater and greater shares of her dignity. Reality TV made her famous because she was normal—just a girl looking for love—and once she became famous, she couldn't imagine going back to being normal again.

FOX apologized for the show, acknowledging the backlash against it, and promised never to do it again. They went on to air shows like *Joe Millionaire*, *Temptation Island*, and *My Big Fat Obnoxious Fiancé*.

The other big networks caught the reality bug, and shows about the search for love have been cranking out ever since. *The Bachelor* is the dominant franchise. The successful and handsome man chooses his bride after slightly more serious consideration than Rick Rockwell's. The would-be spouses spend several weeks with the groom-to-be (or bride-to-be, as the show has bifurcated into both male-centric and female-centric editions), with one contestant eliminated every few days at a "rose ceremony." But of course the dates and encounters are carefully programmed, as is the casting. Ultimately, a show like *The Bachelor* is developed with very little real concern for the contestants. It seems to me that the execs who produce it couldn't care less about the search for love; it's all about the audience. It's all about you and me.

We're captivated by something that is on one hand voyeuristic and judgmental, and on the other hand, a kind of creational hope. We want to believe in love. Many in the audience come up empty in their own searches, and the strange world of reality TV, soap operas, and sitcom romances offers a way of experiencing that desire fulfilled, even if it is packaged, edited, and delivered second hand.

The beauty of a reality show is that it ends. The two get engaged or married, and they are whisked away to their honeymoon as the credits roll. We don't have to watch any of that messy, learning-to-live-together stuff.

THE END OF LOVE STORIES

I find it interesting that in romantic comedies, sitcoms, and reality shows, the end of the story usually occurs in the moments after the wedding. *30 Rock* ended with Liz finding a husband and adopting children. *How I Met Your Mother* will end with Ted meeting his wife. *Friends* ended with Ross (David Schwimmer) and Rachel (Jennifer Aniston) finally getting together. The list goes on and on.

Stories with weddings at the beginning (or even in the middle) necessarily have a very different arc. Genesis 2, our prototype of the search for love, is of course followed by Genesis 3, and we all know how that went. The story of a marriage is always more harsh, more full of trouble. More difficult to tell.

To believe that the search for love ends with everyone feeling "happy ever after" requires a suspension of reality—something we need for most of the stories we tell. In truth, we're well aware that love does not ultimately satisfy the needs of our broken hearts.

Joan Didion once said, "We tell ourselves stories in order to live"[6]—a statement that carries an awful weight of skepticism and despair. These love stories, she might say, are a grasping way that we cling to hope for love even while the real love stories around us disappoint and crumble. We tell them because we need a reason to hope. To believe. To get out of bed in the morning.

But the Bible doesn't let Genesis 2 or Genesis 3 have the last word on life or love. Ultimately, the sacrifice of Adam's rib for the creation of his bride is only a sign that points to a greater sacrifice and a greater union. That greater story tells of a Man who rescues his bride by laying down his life, making her new, and ultimately restoring all things.

Maybe underneath all of the tendencies toward gossip and voyeurism, the fairy-tale fantasies, and the oversold exploits of people searching for love, there's a thread in the human heart that can't give up the belief that one day, true love will come along.

5

O, HOW THE MIGHTY HAVE FALLEN

We're flawed because we want so much more. We're ruined because we get these things and wish for what we had.

Don Draper, *Mad Men*

You don't have to look far to see that the world is full of tragic stories. One half-hour's worth of evening news should be enough to convince us that, indeed, the world can be a frightful and terrible place. Even as I write, Moore, Oklahoma, is picking up the aftermath of a devastating series of storms and tornadoes. You can't see the image of a father looking for a child in the flattened wreckage of an elementary school without thinking, "This isn't the way the world was meant to be."

And that's the truth. The world wasn't meant for death and decay. It wasn't intended for destruction and chaos. It wasn't meant to be full of stories of tragedy and hardship. It was meant to be a place of life and harmony, where God and mankind lived in deep fellowship and community.

I think some flicker of that knowledge remains inside all of our hearts. We know that the world was meant to be different, and when tragedy strikes, we can't help but wonder why. Why did this happen? How did we find ourselves here?

The biblical answer to that question is clear. In Genesis 3, Adam and Eve violate the one prohibition they'd been given by God, dining with the Devil at the tree of knowledge of good and evil, and in the aftermath, all hell—quite literally—breaks loose on the world. The creation is cursed and lashes out against us with thorns and thistles. The elements that we lived with in harmony are now hostile.

For Adam and Eve, the depths of sin's consequences are immediate and far-reaching. Not only must they endure exile from the garden, but also soon after, they see the seeds of their sin bear fruit in their own son, who murders his brother out of envy and spite.

For us, those consequences are all too familiar, as well. We see them on the evening news, and we see them in our lives. We feel the tragic impact of sin in our own sense of loneliness and in the wounds and scars inflicted by others and ourselves. We feel it in our own double-mindedness, in cycles of addiction, and in patterns we wish we could break. We feel it in a looming fear that grips us when terror alerts heighten, when driving through a dangerous neighborhood (or perhaps living in that neighborhood), when bullied by a boss or a coworker, or when our own anger grows beyond the fences of our self-control.

The sense of this tension is universal, and storytellers have sought to account for its presence for generations. Some have sought to explain its origins, as in the myth of Prometheus, who dared to steal fire from the gods, which both empowered and alienated humanity. This ancient story echoes Genesis 3: mankind steals something forbidden, which opens new worlds to them while also incurring the wrath of their God.

Star Wars episodes 1–3 are just such a fall story, too, tracing the descent of Anakin Skywalker (Haden Christensen) from a promising Padawan apprentice to a full-fledged Sith Lord.

He's entranced by the power of the dark side, and eventually compromises everything in order to gain that kind of power.

The aptly titled film *Prometheus*, Ridley Scott's loose prequel to the Alien franchise, is also an exploration of origins and fallenness. In it, the ship *Prometheus* travels to a distant moon as part of a quest for clues to the origins of humanity. But what the crew discovers is something far more dreadful.

The planet is abandoned, with ancient and fossilized remnants of a military installation from the "Engineers"—the aliens they believe created mankind. An exploration of the installation ensues, and bad things start happening at once. Peter Weyland (Guy Pearce), the billionaire financier for the mission, is discovered aboard the ship with ulterior motives: he came on the mission hoping to convince the Engineers to give him a way to extend his life.

The crew's search for knowledge and power leads instead to the discovery of a terrible biological weapon that seems destined to destroy all of them and humanity itself. Here, the Promethean myth is reinterpreted. The powers that they discover bring only disaster, and, one would assume, result in all the horrors that befall Lt. Ellen Ripley and her companions years later.

We think of yet another Greek myth of fallenness: Pandora's box. Zeus created Pandora as a vengeful gift for Epimetheus, with whom he had an ongoing bitterness. As a wedding present, Zeus gave Pandora a beautiful locked box that she was never to open. Zeus gave the key to Epimetheus and warned him never to open it, believing that he almost certainly would. Instead, Pandora stole the key and opened the box, her curiosity becoming far too much for her to handle. In it was every imaginable vice and evil: disease, hatred, bitterness, famine, strife, murder, and war. The world has been a mess ever since.

CHANNEL SURFING
Suffering and *The Tree of Life*

Terrence Mallick's *The Tree of Life* is a polarizing film. It's two hours and nineteen minutes that feels much more like a visual art installation than a movie. For some, Mallick's slow, impressionistic journey is a snooze-fest. For others, it's high art. For me, it remains one of the most beautiful and challenging things I've ever seen.

The film opens with a quotation from the book of Job: "Where were you when I laid the foundations of the earth? . . . When the morning stars sang together and all the sons of God shouted for joy?" (Job 38:4, 7). From there, it juxtaposes the story of creation with a family's story of loss and suffering. Mallick journeys through the evolution of the world, with subtle meditations on death, tragedy, and violence. Against that backdrop is the story of the O'Brien family, an archetypical twentieth-century American family living in Waco, Texas. As the story unfolds, the O'Briens suffer—losing two sons (one to a pool accident, the other to Vietnam).

It's an echo of Job's story. Job suffered terrible tragedy, losing his children as well, and he expected God to show up and give him answers as to why. Instead, God beautifully humbles Job by recounting his handiwork in making the world. Theologian Belden Lane describes God's response like this:

> When God finally speaks out of the whirlwind, it is to conduct a tour of the harsh Palestinian countryside. God points to the wine-dark sea, the towering clouds over a desolate land, the storehouses of snow and hail in the distant mountains. God asks Job what all this has to do with him.

Does the wild ox pay him any attention? . . . Does Leviathan speak to him a single word? . . .

In the silence that's left when the whirl-wind subsides, Job finds what he'd sought all along. . . . Job is given no answer, but in being drawn out of himself, he's met by God.[1]

In *The Tree of Life*, Sean Penn plays Jack O'Brien, the grown son of the O'Brien family who seems tortured by the loss of his brothers and the emotional distance of his harsh father. As the film progresses, we journey with Jack through his memories, juxtaposed with images of creation that serve to illustrate God's speech to Job, and by the film's end, Jack comes to a place of freedom.

The message of *The Tree of Life* is that there are two ways through this world. The first is the way of nature, and it's a harsh existence, subjected to forces much bigger than us and destined for suffering. Jack O'Brien's father (Brad Pitt) personifies this way, pushing his kids to be hard and strong. But ultimately, the way of nature crushes him. The other is the way of grace, personified by the O'Briens' mother (Jessica Chastain), whose nurturing and love is otherworldly. Through his memories of her, Jack comes to terms with his loss and transcends the darkness. He walks in a sort of dream state through a vacant desert, to an open door, and through it to a beautiful shoreline where his family awaits him amid a thousand other re-unions, all ushered together by angelic presences.

Like Job, Jack comes to sense his smallness against the scale of creation, and yet he knows—through the gracious love of his mother—that his life matters to God, that he hasn't gone unnoticed, and though he has no answers for why, he has joy and hope that transcends.

What apt metaphors such stories are for Genesis 3. How swiftly the world falls into chaos. How sharp the contrast is between the world before and after the fall.

But there are also important distinctions. The fall isn't mere myth, and it's not just about the introduction or discovery of evil. Rather, it's the story of a broken relationship, and its consequences are inherently relational. We have become disconnected from the One who gives us meaning, whose image we bear. Augustine put it well when he said, "O crooked ways! Woe to the audacious soul which hoped that by forsaking thee it would find some better thing! It tossed and turned upon back and side and belly—but the bed is hard and thou alone givest it rest."[2] Or as he said elsewhere, "Thou hast made us for thyself, and restless is our heart until it comes to rest in thee."[3]

That sense of restlessness and alienation pervades our fall stories. The television series *Lost* was, in many ways, a fall story. Each character was introduced as a castaway, and much of the series was spent searching backwards through their stories. We discovered that they were all "lost" long before the plane crashed on the island, living lonesome lives of exile and twisted identity. This exploration of backstory created a dense complexity to the show, and it was the beauty of *Lost*. The characters developed in ways that left the audience perpetually off-balance, rendering them at times sympathetic and at times contemptible. Jack (Matthew Fox) appears as a Boy Scout until we see him as a drunk. Locke (Terry O'Quinn) appears as powerful and formidable until we discover that he's spent years confined to a wheelchair, and the island has restored his ability to walk. Even Hurley (Jorge Garcia), who seemed the most likable and least shadowy character on the show, had a dark past. In fact, much of the mystery and magic on the show could be traced to his one flaw: he opened a sort of Pandora's box when he chose to use a cursed set of numbers for a lottery ticket. He won, and everything in his life fell apart afterward.

FALLING WITH *MAD MEN*

Perhaps the most expansive meditation on the fall in contemporary culture is *Mad Men*, created by Matthew Weiner and starring Jon Hamm. *Mad Men* tells the stories of a collection of characters connected through a Madison Avenue advertising agency. It's a grim exploration of identity, alienation, sexual politics, masculinity, seduction, and creativity (to name just a few themes). In short, it's a show about what it means to be human in a fallen world, set in the nostalgic, glamorous, and historically dense backdrop of New York in the 1960s.

All that makes *Mad Men* compelling was revealed—often in hints and whispers—in the first episode of the show. It opens with Don Draper (Jon Hamm) sitting in the midst of a noisy bar, drinking Old Fashioneds and writing busily on a paper napkin. He's stuck on a problem: how do you advertise cigarettes now that their health claims have been thoroughly debunked and the product has been linked to cancer? How do you sell a poisonous lie?

He interviews a waiter about the problem, asking why he smokes his brand. He then sets off to an apartment where we meet Midge (Rosemarie DeWitt), a beautiful artist with whom Don shares his thoughts, a drink, and her bed. At one point he says, "We should get married."[4] Midge laughs it off, saying she doesn't want to be the future ex–Mrs. Draper, and Don heads off to work, still stuck, still swimming in despair over his problem. By that afternoon, he has to have an advertising pitch to give to Lucky Strike, one of his firm's biggest clients.

The scene cuts to Don's office building, where Peggy (Elisabeth Moss) is showing up for her first day of work at Sterling Cooper—the ad agency where Don is the creative director. She gets on the elevator with three young ad execs, who lob a variety of lewd comments at her, and then is quickly introduced to Joan Holloway (Christina Hendricks), the red-headed bombshell who runs the secretarial pool at the office. Joan tells Peggy that the men in the office don't really want a secretary; most of the time they want something in between a mother and a waitress. The rest of the time . . .

The implication is clear. Peggy is told to wear shorter skirts to show off her "cute ankles" and to spend some time in front of a mirror, undressed, with a paper bag punched with holes for her eyes over her head. Evaluate her assets. Dress accordingly. She's then sent off to an ob-gyn to get an exam and a prescription for birth control pills.

Pete Campbell (Vincent Kartheiser) enters the scene early on, as well. Pete is a vile young ad exec who is about to get married, and this happens to be the day of his bachelor's party. It's clear that he has one thing on his mind. Pete wants to be like Don, a successful lady-killer and ad exec, but he lacks Don's creative genius and charm. The contempt between the two of them is palpable. Don is disgusted by him, and dismissive. Pete is ambitious and conniving, eager for a chance to climb the next rung on the ladder.

At one point, Pete makes a number of sexually charged comments about Peggy, for which Don berates him: "I bet the whole world looks like one big brassiere strap, waiting to be snapped. . . . Campbell, we're both men here so I'm going to be direct. . . . Advertising is a very small world, and when you do something like malign the reputation of a girl from the steno pool on her first day, you make it even smaller. Keep it up and even if you do get my job, you'll never run this place. You'll die in that corner office a mid level executive with a little bit of hair that women go home with out of pity. Do you want to know why? Because no one will like you."[5]

The advertisers have a terrible first meeting with Rachel Menken (Maggie Siff), the owner of a department store who's considering changing ad agencies and hiring Sterling Cooper (the meeting is punctuated by a host of anti-Semitic side comments between Don and Roger Sterling [John Slattery], one of the agency's partners), and Don is soon back in his office mulling over the meeting with Lucky Strike. Losing this client will be disastrous.

When the meeting finally occurs, the entire Sterling Cooper team flounders. The owners of Lucky Strike are appalled by the hassle they're getting from the government about their product, and the agency has no workable ideas for helping get their reputation back in the market. People now think "cancer" when they hear "cigarettes."

Lucky Strike is standing to walk out of the room, when Don suddenly gets a spark of inspiration. He walks to a chalkboard, calls Lucky Strike back, and pitches a new idea. It's a trademark for him on the show—a moment of brilliant, creative wordplay and imagination that is the source of his reputation as the best creative director in the ad business. He's spectacular—seductive, winsome, and compelling—and the clients leave happy.

There's a brief celebration, and soon the younger men are off to Pete's bachelor party. Don invites Rachel Menken out to dinner to apologize for his rudeness earlier, and begins working that seductive skill on her, as well.

Their conversation turns to why Rachel isn't married. At first she's indignant for being asked. Is it wrong that she loves work? Is it wrong that she wants to make her father's business all that it can be? Then she adds that it's because: "I've never been in love."

Don mocks her, saying, "She isn't married because she's never been in love. I think I wrote that just to sell nylons."

Don doesn't believe in love. He believes in the facade of advertising. He believes in seduction. He believes in manipulation. He goes on to describe what people *think* love is, and you can tell he hits a nerve with Menken, describing the marriage, family, and romance she indeed longs for. "The reason you haven't felt it is because it doesn't exist," Don concludes. "What you call 'love' was invented by guys like me. To sell nylons."

"Is that right?" Rachel says.

"Pretty sure about it. You're born alone and you die alone and this world just drops a bunch of rules on top of you to make you forget those facts, but I never forget. I'm living like there's no tomorrow because there isn't one."

Rachel's reply is loaded: "I don't think I realized it until this moment, but it must be hard being a man too."

"Excuse me?"

"Mr. Draper . . ."

"Don."

"Mr. Draper, I don't know what it is you really believe in, but I do know what it feels like to be out of place. To be disconnected. To see the whole world laid out in front of you, the way other people live it. . . . There's something about you that tells me that you know it too."

"I don't know that that's true."[6] Don says, but it's obvious he does.

Rachel speaks from her social and cultural alienation. She's a woman in a decidedly chauvinistic world, and she's Jewish. Two strikes against her ability to be accepted in the WASPish world of New York high society. She's continually experiencing life as an outsider looking in, despite her beauty, despite the success of the department store, despite her wealth.

She's able to see, through Don's cold exterior, that he knows that feeling. He, too, has been an outsider looking in, and in spite of his nihilistic professions, he knows loneliness and isolation. All is not glamour, seduction, and success.

Rachel agrees to work with Sterling Cooper, and they part ways. The camera then takes us to the exterior of Peggy's apartment, where Pete Campbell is drunkenly hammering on her front door. It's clear what he wants; his bachelor party was a bust for him, and no woman wanted anything to do with him. But Peggy's been told that this is her path to success in the office, and despite the fact that she finds him despicable, she takes him to her bed. The consequences aren't discovered for many episodes.

The show cuts back to Don, on a train, driving a car, then arriving at the front door of a big, beautiful suburban home with white walls and a red front door. As he enters, a light switches on upstairs, revealing Betty (January Jones)—Don's wife. Soon we also see his two sleeping children.

For those who've been watching the show for several seasons, you've probably forgotten the shock of this moment. But when I first watched the episode, I felt as though the final minute of the show reinterpreted everything we'd seen before: Don's conversations with Midge, his berating of Pete, his confrontation with Rachel. Everything becomes confused and murky when we learn he's a husband and a father. He's living in two different worlds. The show ends with a shot of Don, sitting on the edge of his daughter's bed, a hand on her back and a hand on his son, sleeping in another bed nearby. Betty stands in the doorway looking on. As the camera pans back and the credits roll, the song "On the Street Where You Live" begins to play—a song from *My Fair Lady* about the intoxicating effects of being close to the one you love.

It's a brilliant "reveal" moment, where we discover that as dark and complicated as things seemed, we were only scratching the surface—especially when it comes to who Don really is.

CHANNEL SURFING
Why Seinfeld's Final Episode Was Perfect

Some readers may be too young to remember, but *Seinfeld*'s final episode was eagerly anticipated. It sits just behind *Cheers* and *Mash* on the list of most-watched series finales of all time. The TV Land network suspended programming while it aired, posting an image of a closed door with a taped-up sign that said, "Gone watchin' *Seinfeld*."

But the episode met with many critical jeers. Larry David, one of the show's creators, returned to help co-write the finale, and many blamed his caustic sense of humor for an episode they saw as harsh and bitter.

The plot centered on an incident in which the principal cast members—Jerry (Jerry Seinfeld), Elaine (Julia Louis-Dreyfuss), George (Jason Alexander), and Kramer (Michael Richards)—head to California. For much of the history of the show, Jerry and George have been trying to get NBC to pick up a sitcom based on Jerry's life. By this episode, they have the green light. On the flight out west, Kramer causes an incident, and the plane has to make an emergency landing in Latham, Massachusetts.

There, they witness the carjacking of an overweight man, and Kramer captures the crime on a camcorder. They don't help, they don't call the police; they just make cracks about his weight. The victim alerts the police and the four end up getting arrested. There's a law that requires bystanders to help in such a situation.

What follows is a trial of the four, parading characters from all nine seasons of the show as witnesses to their despicable character.

I think this ending was perfect. The genius of the

show was its ability to make these four incredibly selfish people watchable. Their pettiness, their destructive relationships, their materialism, their conniving and feuding—it had all been fodder for laughs for nine years. They acted as people without consciences, with an unspoken social contract of tolerance for one another, and with little in the way of loyalty or concern for anyone else on the show. And the finale judged them for their sins.

The episode ends with the judge throwing the book at them, saying, "I do not know how or under what circumstances the four of you found each other, but your callous indifference and utter disregard for everything that is good and decent has rocked the very foundation upon which our society is built. I can think of nothing more fitting than for the four of you to spend a year removed from society so that you can contemplate the manner in which you have conducted yourselves."[7]

Interestingly, the show ends cyclically. In the jail cell, Jerry initiates a conversation with George about shirt buttons that's identical to a conversation they had on the show's first episode. George responds, "Haven't we had this conversation before?" The conversation stops, and the camera pans back slowly, leaving the four in the cell in silence.

Comedy often thrives on the antics of the fool. In *Seinfeld*, the fools are self-absorbed, judgmental, and malicious New Yorkers, and for nine years we laughed at them. In this final episode, Larry David and Jerry Seinfeld pull back the lenses a bit, showing us a wide-angle view of the show, and they remind us of all that we laughed at. By judging the characters, the audience who laughed along is implicated too, and maybe that's what made the episode so unpopular.

ORIGINAL SINS

As the show progresses, we see Don's story told through a variety of flashbacks and odd, chance encounters. Not only is he living two lives (as a cosmopolitan, lady-killing ad exec in Manhattan and as a dutiful husband and father in the suburbs), but we discover that he isn't actually Don Draper at all. His name is Dick Whitman. While deployed in the Korean War, he switched identities with a man who died next to him during some shelling—a man named Don Draper. Whitman was just beginning his deployment, and Draper was at the end of his. So he switched dog tags with the dead man, spent some time recovering at an army hospital, and returned to the States a new man, avoiding the war and leaving his past behind.

It was a lie that held promise and hope—a new life and a new identity. He was leaving behind the life an outsider, the life Rachel Mencken saw in his eyes over dinner. It turns out that this tall, dark, handsome ad man is actually the bastard son of a poor farmer and a prostitute. He grew up despised by his stepmother and a constant reminder of regret to his father. By seizing a new life, a new name, he had hope for a new future.

But like all lies, it came with terrible consequences. The real Draper was married, and Don had to find a way to deal with his wife. He also had relationships and connections to his past that would inevitably come back to haunt him. Though he seems to only want to live for today, "move forward" as he often says, he can't escape his past and his true, broken identity.

Like all lies, it birthed more, and by the time we meet Don in the show's pilot, he's absolutely swimming in them. Over the seasons that have followed, we've watched them result in one terrible consequence after another.

Season 1 has an interesting set of bookends related to Don.

By the time it ends, we've seen him cycle through affairs, reject his past, and begin to lose his marriage. In the final episode of the season, he's pitching an ad campaign for Kodak's new slide projector. During the pitch, he talks about how in advertising, everyone thinks the most powerful word is *new*; it's not—there's something deeper. *Nostalgia.*

He delivers this speech to a room full of execs from Kodak and Sterling Cooper, speaking slowly and cycling through pictures of his own family: scenes of him playing with his kids, climbing trees, opening Christmas presents, each slide going back further and further through time, showing the children younger and younger, showing Don and Betty as new parents and newlyweds, hopelessly in love. The scenes—like most family photos—are idyllic.

"In Greek," Don says, "*nostalgia* literally means the pain from an old wound. It's a twinge in your heart, far more powerful than memory alone. This device isn't a spaceship; it's a time machine. It goes backwards, forwards. It takes us to a place where we ache to go again. It's not called the wheel; it's called the carousel. It lets us travel the way a child travels, around and around and back home again, to a place where you know you are loved."[8]

It's stirring. By the end, even these cynical ad men are moved. One gets up and leaves the room, emotionally wrecked. Don, of course, wins the account, but moreover, he seems to make (if only in his mind) a renewed commitment to his family. Betty and the kids were leaving for Thanksgiving, and he had planned on missing the holiday for work. Now, renewed in his commitment to them, he heads home on the train.

We see a side of Don that doesn't simply believe you're born alone and you die alone. Something in him still longs for connection, for family, for continuity.

We see him walk through the door of his home later, surprising the family before they leave for the train station. Betty's face warms, the kids yell "Daddy," and everything seems hopeful again for the Drapers as he announces that he's going with them. But suddenly the scene cuts back to Don opening the door. What happened before was a scenario he played out in his mind. Instead, he opens the door to an empty house. He's too late; they've gone. The camera angle is identical to the night Don comes home in episode 1, where we first discover he's married. Now, he stands alone at the bottom of the stair, eventually slumping on a step. The nostalgic wound is throbbing.

Don isn't the only one whose sins are finding him out on *Mad Men*. In fact, it's hard to find anyone on the show that isn't in some way living a lie and suffering the consequences. Peggy and Pete's sexual encounter on the first episode (which isn't the only one between them) leads to another of *Mad Men*'s trademark surprises.

In the same episode that Don wins the Kodak account (season 1's finale), Pete lands an account with Clearasil—a company that happens to be owned by his father-in-law. Peggy meanwhile has only become more hostile with Pete, and more liked and trusted by Don. She was invaluable on an earlier campaign, and now Don wants to promote her from the secretarial pool to junior ad copywriter.

Peggy is, of course, delighted and honored, and Pete is angry that a woman would be given an account so personally important to him. It adds insult to injury that the woman in question is Peggy, who has now spurned Pete.

As Peggy moves into her new office (enduring some biting comments from Joan, who is jealous as well), she breaks a sweat and begins to feel terrible, heading to the hospital. There, she discovers she's not only pregnant, but in labor, and she collapses. Here, at the moment of her great triumph at work—something she's hoped for and strived for with bold ambition as a woman in the workplace—she becomes a mother, something her ambition simply cannot bear. How can she continue her climb and raise a child?

She ends up having a psychological breakdown, and she's kept in the hospital for several weeks. The blend of shock from her pregnancy and internal conflict about being a mother leaves her in a state of denial that is almost catatonic, and the doctors can't break through.

In an episode called "The New Girl" from season 2, we see a flashback to a conversation between Don and Peggy from that time in the hospital. Peggy disappeared from her office for weeks after the promotion, and when Don talked to her mother, he was told she had tuberculosis. This didn't comfort him, and he sought her out in the hospital, finding her in the psychiatric ward instead.

"What's wrong with you?" he asks.

"I don't know," Peggy said.

"What do they want you to do?"

"I don't know."

"Yes, you do. Do it. Do whatever they say." He leans forward. "Peggy, listen to me. Get out of here and move forward. This never happened. It will shock you how much it never happened."[9]

This is Don's philosophy. It near-perfectly describes his whole way of living and being in the world. He has spent his entire life running from his past, denying it, burying it, pretending it never happened, and at the time that he tells her this, his counsel has proven true. He's had few consequences for his secrets.

Peggy gives up the baby for adoption, heads back to work, and pretends it all never happened. Don, in a strange expression of loyalty, covers for her with the rest of the office. Unlike Don, Peggy carries the wound a bit more visibly on the show. In one moment, she describes the sense of inner vacancy, saying, "Well, one day you're there, and then all of a sudden, there's less of you. And you wonder where that part went. If it's living somewhere outside of you. And you keep thinking maybe you'll get it back. And then you realize it's just gone."[10]

Sin is costly. It takes a piece of us and leaves us with a hard-to-articulate feeling of longing and brokenness—a sense that there's a hollow spot inside our souls.

THE COMPLEXITY OF SIN

Part of what makes *Mad Men* so compelling (and this is true of almost any tragedy or drama) is that it maintains a delicate balance between exposing the character's flaws and eliciting the audience's sympathy. Don's sins are despicable, but somehow the audience still feels as though they're on his side—especially in his work. He's brilliant and eloquent, and he's often the only one in the office who treats women with a sense of worth. He raises Peggy from being a secretary to being a top writer and part of the creative team. Joan Holloway receives endless harassment and advances from other men, but Don always shows her the utmost respect.

As Luther would say, we're sinners and saints all at once. Even the lowest of sinners is capable, at times, of glorious good deeds and brilliant works. We are image-bearers, and we can't help but cast off reflections of God's glory—as dim and pale as they may be—throughout our lives. Our faded glory punctuates the tragedy of Genesis 3, reminding us how the world might have been had sin not shattered everything, and it fills many in the world with an insatiable angst when they see what might have been. That possibility haunts *Mad Men*, too. Don knows that he's selling lies, but his unique gift is getting beyond thinking and talking about products to thinking and talking about the deep longing that sits behind them. Advertising works when it taps into deep human desire, offering redemptive hopes that sell products that can never deliver on the promise. We long for love, for community, for beauty, and for happiness, and Don Draper knows how to cut through the din of marketing and tap into those longings. He makes his name selling false hopes for redemption and happiness.

But he isn't a mere monster. Rightly viewed, the world after Genesis 3 (and its human inhabitants) isn't simply condemnable; it's also pitiable. God himself—the only righteous Judge of the world—shows mercy again and again to sinners, clothing Adam and Eve, marking Cain, preserving Noah, Isaac, Lot, Israel, and of course, you and me. Sin has unleashed upon the world a host of troubles and sorrows, alienating us from God and from all of the good things that flow from him—all of the longings described above. We endure a world wherein we're separated from these good gifts, and our souls bear the scars of that separation.

Consider that Don Draper didn't ask to be born. He arrived in the world the son of a farmer and a prostitute who died at birth. His father, too, died when Don was still very young, after being kicked by a horse that was frightened by a thunderclap. His stepmother despised him, as he was a constant reminder of her husband's infidelity, and she reluctantly raised him, taking him along to live in a brothel where she worked (not as a prostitute, though) after his father's death.

In an episode titled "The Crash," we see flashbacks of Don's life in the brothel. Young Don—maybe thirteen to fifteen years old—is sick with a nagging cough and fevers. His stepmother shows no interest in helping him recover, and sends him to the attic with a bedroll. On his way there, a young prostitute pulls him into her room, checks him out, and lets him know that he's going to be okay. She puts him in her bed and nurses him back to health—the only nurturing that we've ever seen in Don's childhood.

But it doesn't end there. Before Don leaves her room, after his fever has broken and he's well, she has sex with him. She's later kicked out of the brothel for holding out on money with the owner, and in the process, she admits to sleeping with Don. The scene ends with a shot of Don, huddled in a corner, while his stepmother mercilessly beats him.

Freud would have a field day.

Who could fault the young hooker for nurturing the sick boy? And who could condone her sleeping with him? No wonder Don's sexual ethics are so mixed. He sees past a culture's objectification of women (like Joan) at least in part because this prostitute—our culture's ultimate example of objectification—showed him care and affection like no one else ever had. And yet his sexual identity is malformed in the process.

Don's alienated childhood leaves him adrift, unable to sustain any real intimacy or love, no matter how much he desires it. Sin unleashes generations of suffering on the world, and its results are complex, leaving individual motivations murky and hard to discern. Its complexity is most evident when we understand one another's stories, and it should result in compassion for one another.

Don's air of power and dominance is also ultimately revealed as a mask for a deeper wound. In "A Man with a Plan," Don is in the middle of an affair with Sylvia Rosen (Linda Cardellini), the wife of a doctor who lives one floor below Don and his second wife, Megan (Jessica Paré). Sylvia and her husband have separated, and Don has her meet him at a hotel room. Once there together, he becomes more demanding and domineering than ever, telling her that she exists only for his pleasure, and she's never to leave the hotel room. Sylvia, uncomfortable, plays along, appearing weak and compliant. He refuses to let her leave the hotel, takes away the book she was reading, and won't tell her when he'll return. He visits her for their trysts, and disappears again. She's to stay undressed and wait for his return.

By the episode's end, Don returns to find Sylvia dressed and ready to walk out the door. At first he's stern and threatening, but Sylvia merely sighs him away. "It's over. This is over," she says, referring not only to their time in the hotel, but the entire affair. Suddenly, Don's voice cracks. The hard exterior is gone, and he barely gets out the word, "Please."[11]

The audience realizes in that moment that Sylvia's been in control the entire time. Don's domineering isn't real; it's an act, the fantasy of a broken man. So long as it was a convenient and exciting escape from her struggling marriage, Sylvia would play along, but now she's done. In the following episode, Don schemes to get her back, and we see him more desperate than ever before.

Few in Don's life see how truly broken he is. Betty doesn't see it until long after they've divorced, and she comments on it when they "hook up" at a summer camp where their son is staying. As they lie in bed talking about their failed marriage and their current spouses, Betty says of Megan, "That poor girl. She doesn't know that loving you is the worst way of getting to you."[12] Betty knows it first hand, having endured the pain of Don's lies and betrayal.

One of the few who got past Don's veneer was Anna Draper (Melinda Page Hamilton), the wife of the real Don Draper, who hunts him down in the years after the war. At first, Don is frightened that she'll expose him as a fraud, but eventually the two become close friends. She knows all of his secrets, and she is happy for him when he marries Betty (legally divorcing Anna in the process). He supports her financially right up until the time of her death of stomach cancer in season 4, an event that crushes Don.

In one of the show's most touching scenes, Don receives the phone call about Anna's death while Peggy is in the room with him. He weeps and says, "She was the only person that really knew me." Peggy places a hand on Don's, and says, "She wasn't the *only* one."[13]

It's a great scene for many reasons. These two have shared much. Don is Peggy's mentor, but they've also become confidants. Don knows about Peggy's child, and Peggy has helped Don out of trouble on a number of occasions. She knows that he's really Dick Whitman. And here, these two broken people find comfort and solidarity in their friendship; they wear no masks before one another.

A similar moment of solidarity comes in season 1. Pete Campbell, in a power play against Don, discovers his false identity. He brings the news to Bert Cooper (Robert Morse), one of the firm's partners, announcing that Don is a fraud, maybe an army deserter, possibly a criminal.

Bert walks across the room and shocks Pete by saying, "Mr. Campbell, who cares? . . . This country was built and run by men with worse stories than you've imagined here. . . . The Japanese have a saying: A man is whatever room he is in and right now, Donald Draper is in this room. I assure you: there is more profit in forgetting this."[14]

Pete leaves the room, and Bert tells Don he can fire him if he'd like, but he cautions against it. "One never knows how loyalty is born."[15] Of course, the true loyalty born in the scene is the loyalty between Don and Bert.

In each of these scenes, someone's sin is exposed, and it's met with solidarity. Bert's comments, veiled as they are, seem to imply a level of understanding that goes beyond whitewashing the accusation; they imply (to this viewer, anyway) that he, too, has his secrets. Bert, like Peggy, is extending grace—not as one in a position of moral superiority, but as a fellow sinner, someone in need of grace himself.

WHY WE LOVE *MAD MEN*

Perhaps this strange grace and solidarity are the key to the show's fanatical following. Why would anyone want to subject themselves to enduring the grueling journey we take with Don, Peggy, and the others? Or for that matter, why would we subject ourselves to the tragedy in *Hamlet* or *The Sopranos*? What keeps us coming back?

There are obvious dramatic answers. Good entertainment involves great writing, acting, directing, and more. Their world is believable and appealing, and it draws us in—that's the power of great art. But that's not the only reason.

We identify. We understand how it feels to keep dark secrets, to feel torn between who we want the world to see and who we know ourselves to truly be. We know the agonizing consequences of bad decisions, and when we see Joan or Peggy or Don or even Pete grinding through them, we can identify. We sense in some small way the solidarity of sinners. As alien as our lives might feel at times, others have felt the same.

There's always a place for tragedy in the stories we tell. In some ways, we watch to know ourselves. How did we get here? Why does everything seem so broken? Is there any hope for redemption?

Often, there's not. I don't think it any kind of coincidence that *Mad Men*'s opening credits feature a silhouette of Don falling out of a skyscraper onto Madison Avenue, surrounded by images from ads that drift past like religious icons—efforts at redemption that do nothing to stop his fall. He's on a collision course with the consequences of his actions, and there's nothing to stop the fall. He can profess to only move forward all he wants, but the past has legs, and it finds him again and again.

Fall stories help orient us to a world that doesn't work out how we expect. They help us to make sense of the ruin we see around us. They help us to know we're not alone in our sorrows and failures, and they point to the deep need we all have for answers, for hope, and for redemption.

We have all lived our own fall stories in one way or another, and most of us hope that they're not the last word on our lives.

6

FRUSTRATION

The game's out there, and it's play or get played.

Omar, *The Wire*

I've often heard people say that life isn't like the movies, and that's certainly true. Love is rarely "happy ever after." Crime often goes unpunished. Underdogs lose the big game. Nerds seldom take off their glasses to reveal a heartthrob, and as Indiana Jones once said, "X never, ever marks the spot."[1] Only in the world of stories are these laws (mostly) reliable.

We love that reliability. It's how we wish the world worked. We want the good guys to win and the couple to drive off into the sunset, happy ever after. Our attitudes about God and religion, too, are shaped by that desire. We want to believe that if we "do good," we will earn God's favor and blessing. Obey the laws, and life goes well. If you avoid the tragic mistakes of protagonists like Hamlet or Don Draper, you'll avoid their downfalls.

But there is the fall, and there is fallenness. There is failure, and there is frustration. Sin's presence in the world isn't visible only in scandalous headlines and gossip; it's visible in the weary, laborious grind that characterizes everyday life.

We often see sin's consequences in random, hard-to-trace, sometimes mind-bogglingly frustrating ways. Suffering in the world isn't easily accounted for, and it certainly isn't understood by the glib, "oh, you must have done something to deserve this" explanation we often give.

Who can say why a child has leukemia? Who can say why a father was killed by a tornado? Who can say why a bystander was killed in a shooting?

For that matter, who can say why a criminal kingpin's reign goes uninterrupted? Why does someone who cheats on his taxes win the lottery? Why do the wicked prosper?

One of the great gifts God has given his people is the Old Testament Wisdom Literature. Job, Ecclesiastes, and Proverbs are extended meditations on life in this fallen, complex world, where injustices often leave us baffled and frustrated.

It was tempting for Israel—as it's tempting for us—to assume that we have control over our circumstances and fates. If we simply obey the law, God owes us. We'll be blessed with health and wealth, regardless of our circumstances.

The Bible's Wisdom Literature tempers those expectations, reminding us that life is complex and unpredictable, and its joys are temporal. The consequences of sin aren't just personal; sin has infected the whole world, and no amount of good behavior or righteousness on our part can exempt us from its wearying reign. Rather than set our hopes on the happiness that can come from pleasure, or status, or even justice and morality, the Wisdom Books invite us to set our hopes on knowing and being known by the God who made us. Simultaneously, they challenge us to lower our expectations, expecting less satisfaction from work, pleasure, status, and success.

> Vanity of vanities, says the Preacher,
>   vanity of vanities! All is vanity.

> What does man gain by all the toil
>> at which he toils under the sun?
> A generation goes, and a generation comes,
>> but the earth remains forever. . . .
> All things are full of weariness;
>> a man cannot utter it;
> the eye is not satisfied with seeing,
>> nor the ear filled with hearing.
> What has been is what will be,
>> and what has been done is what will be done,
>> and there is nothing new under the sun.
>> (Eccles. 1:2–4, 8–9)

According to the author of Ecclesiastes, life has a sense of inevitability, frustration, and pointlessness. Our efforts disappoint. Feasts fill us temporarily. Success is short-lived. We build empires and then watch someone else take them over. Our sexual appetites can be fulfilled only temporarily. We are insatiable.

This experience of frustration isn't limited to Christians and Jews. In ordinary life, all people experience it in things like injustice in the marketplace and broken political and justice systems. We also experience it as brutal monotony. Have you ever had a job that felt mindless and soul-sucking? A daily grind that left you wondering, "What have I done with my life?"

Herman Melville's short story *Bartleby, the Scrivener* is a classic reflection on this sort of monotony, telling the story of an office clerk hired by a law firm. The office was dysfunctional to begin with, employing two scriveners (who copy legal documents by hand) that can each work only half a day: one because he suffers from an irritable stomach, the other because he's a drunk. Bartleby is hired to help with the work and hopefully temper the other two employees, but soon he begins to answer every request with the phrase, "I would prefer not to."[2]

He stops working but refuses to leave the office, sleeping in a corner and answering every request with the same phrase. The lawyer, exasperated by Bartleby's pitiable depression, moves out of the office, and soon the new tenants are asking for his help in removing Bartleby. He's sleeping in the stairwell and on the front steps until he's dragged off to a prison called the Tombs. There, the lawyer bribes the guard to make sure he's well cared for, but Bartleby eventually prefers not to eat and dies of starvation. It's revealed that he previously worked in a "dead letter" office, the place where the post office sends undeliverable mail, and one is left to conclude that he was driven to despair because of life's ultimate futility.

Bartleby's story resounds in many stories about bureaucracy. We find it in early scenes of the Coen brothers' *The Hudsucker Proxy*, and it inspired Stephen King's *Bag of Bones*. *Bartleby* is the name of one of the despairing angels in Kevin Smith's *Dogma*, who convinced the Angel of Death to quit his job one day.

But perhaps we see Bartleby most clearly in Mike Judge's movie *Office Space*, where Peter Gibbons (Ron Livingston) suffers a meaningless, soul-sucking job, and one day decides not to go anymore. He doesn't quit. He occasionally shows up at the office (to dismantle his cubicle and clean a bass on his desktop), but he isn't planning on doing any work. Unlike Bartleby, Peter's frustration and sense of futility result in a promotion and a raise, further underlining the absurdity and pointlessness of the work.

These stories all ask the same questions. Why? What's the point? Why go on? Why show up? They answer in various ways. *Office Space* ends with an odd sort of homage to community and love. The American version of *The Office* (which explored similar themes) ends in a similar way. *The Hudsucker Proxy* offers hope in the way of love, creativity, and imagination. Oddly enough, it's *Dogma*—which is by far the most crass and offensive of the examples—that ends on a note similar to Ecclesiastes: knowing and being known by God is the only real hope in life.

Apart from such an answer, honest explorations about the way the world works often end in despair.

PLAYING THE GAME: *THE WIRE* AS ECCLESIASTES

Perhaps the most significant, long-term exploration of life's futility is the HBO drama *The Wire*, a show about the city of Baltimore as seen through its police, politicians, drug dealers, and blue-collar citizens.

Most police dramas are morality tales, where a crime is committed by some miscreant and ultimately brought to justice by intrepid, dogged, mildly flawed detectives. This accurately describes shows like *NYPD Blue*, *Homicide*, the *CSI* franchise, and many others that have come and gone over the years.

The Wire is something altogether different. Over the course of five seasons and sixty episodes, it explores the interrelated nature of drug money, politics, and police work. It's told from the perspective of both the police and the criminals, and the writers have a knack for exposing the humanity of everyone involved. There are no superheroes or supervillains; there are only humans, image-bearers, at once brilliant and terrible, loveable and loathable.

The Wire has garnered a cult-like following, with many viewers discovering it years after it went off the air (via online streaming and DVDs). Many critics call it the greatest show of all time, and Ivy League schools teach classes about it, exploring its sociological, racial, political, and literary implications.

Its central premise—I believe—is in concert with Ecclesiastes. Life is vanity. Frustration. A chasing of the wind (Eccles. 2:26). Whether cop or criminal, CEO or crime boss, life is just a game, and these various categories are all just different ways of playing it.

The mind behind the show is David Simon, a former *Baltimore Sun* crime reporter who wrote for *Homicide: Life on the Street* and went on to create *Generation Kill*, an HBO miniseries about the war in Iraq, and *Treme*, another HBO series about the aftermath of Hurricane Katrina. Rather than the write in the episodic form of most procedural dramas, *The Wire* is a kind of character study—with each episode unfolding the lives of the characters and ultimately the life of Baltimore itself. Some of the story lines stretch over the entire show's narrative, finding resolution only at the end of the final season (if you can even call it "resolution").

Rather than look at separate plot points, one can examine the individual lives of the characters and hear the echoes of Ecclesiastes' Teacher: all of life is a chasing of the wind.

"LIFE JUST BE THAT WAY"

We meet Detective Jimmy McNulty (Dominic West) on the stoop of a Baltimore brownstone, interviewing a young thug in the aftermath of a gang shooting. The two sit in the warm glow of the street lamps, yards away from a dead body, a pool of blood, and a shocked crowd that watches wide-eyed, whispering, gossiping. Flickering lights from police cars highlight their faces while they talk about the dead kid and his unfortunate nickname, Snot.

McNulty offers a commentary on the name—how the kid probably forgot his jacket one day, his nose ran, and someone pinned him with that name for life. Unfair, isn't it? "Life just be that way," the kid next to him says.

Every week, it turns out, Snot would hang out at an alley craps game, wait until the pot got big, grab the cash, and run for it. Every week. Even so, the kid says, they didn't have to kill him. They could have just beat him up, like they normally did.

"I gotta ask you," McNulty says. "If every time, Snot Boogie would grab the money and run away, why'dja even let him in the game?"

"Got to," says the kid. "This is America."[3]

The camera cuts to a shot of Snot's dead face looking the camera in the eye, with McNulty and the thug in the background, and the opening theme begins.

In a weird way, this is prototypical of everything that *The Wire* is about. It's not a show in which justice plays out in neat and tidy lines, where there are heroes (or antiheroes) and villains; instead, there is random, senseless violence. Stupid violence, occurring in ways that are patternless, unpredictable, and meaningless, like a kid getting a terrible nickname on a cold Baltimore day.

Though in many ways McNulty fits the mold of the classic TV homicide detective—tall, handsome, tough, and wisecracking—in many other ways, he's a disaster. McNulty has a deep disdain for authority, and his superiors grow to truly hate him.

While he wants justice, they want good stats—crimes that are easily solved and quickly taken off their desks. It's a plague throughout the show that the police department would rather have short investigations and quick busts of low-level thugs than invest time and resources to catch the criminals at the center of power in Baltimore. So cops spend their days rounding up the same old crews—kids that work corners and junkies that possess a few doses of heroin—instead of actually building cases against the powers behind the drugs. The priority on homicides isn't justice, but clearance rates. Moving from "red" to "black," from unsolved to solved as quickly as possible.

CHANNEL SURFING
Frustration and Complex Social Issues

Some social issues feel overwhelming and complex. They are often more difficult to describe than they are to depict, and stories have a way of helping us to experience their complexity and frustration.

One of the best examples of this comes from the movie *Crash*. It comes in a telling dialogue between Anthony (Ludacris) and Peter (Larenz Tate), two black men on the streets of Los Angeles. As a white couple passes them on the sidewalk, the wife grips her husband's arm tightly and presses in, pulling back from Anthony and Peter. Anthony is offended by her reaction:

> Anthony: Look around! You couldn't find a whiter, safer or better-lit part of this city. But this white woman sees two black guys, who look like UCLA students, strolling down the sidewalk and her reaction is blind fear. I mean, look at us! Are we dressed like gang-bangers? Huh? No. Do we look threatening? No. Fact, if anybody should be scared around here, it's us: We're the only two black faces surrounded by a sea of over-caffeinated white people, patrolled by the trigger-happy LAPD. So you tell me, why aren't we scared?
>
> Peter: Because we have guns?
>
> Anthony: You could be right.[4]

If you've seen the movie, you know what comes next. Anthony and Peter pull guns, follow the couple down the street, and carjack them. They simultaneously express offense by the stereotype and live it out.

There's a circular logic to the problem. Which comes first? The stereotyping, or the thuggery?

In the words of the Teacher in Ecclesiastes, this too is meaningless, this too is frustration, a chasing of the wind.

The cops face a terrible choice: they can do good police work or make their bosses happy. Most choose to make the bosses happy, taking the easy busts and doing all they can to make unsolved murders go away (by classifying them as suicides, for instance) or finding an excuse to shuffle them off to other departments.

Not McNulty, though.

When the brass wants to end an investigation prematurely, he leaks word to a judge with political influence, or to the press, which threatens to make the department look bad. When a body washes up in the harbor and the police want to shuffle it off to someone else's jurisdiction, McNulty faxes all of the departments a tide report to prove the murder happened in Baltimore's waters. They all know that he's a brilliant investigator, but his insubordination makes them furious.

It also leads to alienation and disgrace. He's demoted from Homicide in season 1 (a role with some sense of prestige) to Harbor Patrol in season 2. His friends trust him less and less as the show goes on, because he simply refuses to work within the lines and confines of the system.

THE COST OF SEEKING JUSTICE

McNulty's personal life parallels his work life. The more intense an investigation becomes, the more out of control his personal life gets. He's never far from a bottle of Jameson whiskey, and in the darkest moments, he's usually got one in his pocket. He and his partner, Bunk (Wendell Pierce), end most of their days in a crummy bar or drinking can after can of beer by a railroad track, swerving through the city's empty streets on their way home.

At the series' beginning, he's separated from his wife and kids, trying to win back her trust. For too many years, he's come home late (or not at all), picking up cocktail waitresses and random girls at bars. He wants a stable life. He wants to be faithful to his wife and present for his sons. But she knows him too well—perhaps better than he knows himself—and refuses to let him get too close.

In many movies, a character like McNulty would be cast as a reformer. His insistence on justice would get results, and by the show's end, the city would be a better place and the department a more honest institution. But *The Wire* wants us to feel tension without any rewards.

McNulty's story takes several odd turns. At the end of season 3, he leaves the Major Investigations division to take a normal patrol job in the Western District. His personal life is a shambles (as usual), and he longs to settle down and have some normality. In season 4, he's a peripheral character, working his patrol, remarried, and appearing as a happy, healthy guy. It seems as though the distance he's put between himself and the investigations, thereby easing the burden of murder, big money, and drug cases, has allowed him to enjoy a normal life. It's an interesting bit of realism, demonstrating the enormous cost one might pay when carrying such burdens.

But for McNulty, the reprieve doesn't last. In season 5, he returns to Major Crimes and takes his insubordination to new, maddened heights. A long-term investigation into a series of execution-style killings in abandoned row houses gets cut short due to budget constraints, and McNulty is incensed. He, along with another rules-bending detective named Lester Freamon (Clarke Peters), begins manipulating the crime scenes around homeless men found dead of exposure or alcohol poisoning, so that they appear to be linked by a single, perverse, serial killer. The thought of such a killer on the loose fills the city with fear, and the department opens up funds for the investigation—which McNulty and Freamon channel toward their now-dead row house investigation.

But McNulty seems to be losing his grip on reality. He's drinking constantly, looking wild-eyed and haggard. His dogged pursuit of Marlo Stanfield (Jamie Hector), the dealer behind these killings, has made him crazy. One can't help but watch this final season of the show with a jaw-dropped sense of disbelief.

At first, McNulty's madness seems to be working. They get phone taps up on some of the dealers, and McNulty is able to help a few other detectives get paid for overtime hours. But soon, too many plates are spinning, and no amount of scheming can keep them going any longer. Everything begins to crash to the ground, especially once Kima Greggs (Sonja Sohn)—one of McNulty's friends on the squad—decides to turn him in.

Even here, though, we're denied a satisfying resolution. Politicians and department heads have too much at stake to allow the whole story to be exposed, so they make McNulty a sort of sacrificial lamb, offer a few bland solutions to the case to the public, and return, as ever, to business as usual. McNulty is forced to quit policing, and the department holds a funeral-themed going away party. Throughout the show, cops who die are treated to a kind of pyre-like celebration at an Irish bar, complete with the corpse, which lies on a pool table while colleagues sing, drink, and tell stories. McNulty's retirement party is a mock funeral, with McNulty lying on the pool table while he's eulogized, mocked, and celebrated.

The only thing that's truly dead, though, is McNulty's faith in justice—his sense that the bad guys "don't get to win." His life's pursuit has proven meaningless.

MEANINGLESSNESS AND *THE WIRE*

The Wire is compelling and surprising because it doesn't follow any predetermined story arc. It doesn't simply reverse the typical resolution of your normal police procedural drama; it scrambles it entirely. So while the quest for meaning via justice is denied to cops like McNulty and Freamon, the quest for meaning via success, power, and money is denied to the politicians and drug dealers as well.

A handful of examples will suffice. Stringer Bell (Idris Elba) and Proposition Joe (Robert F. Chew) are two key figures in the Baltimore drug business. They both have an interest in expanding and stabilizing the drug trade, ending the wars between dealers, and running effective organizations. Stringer takes classes in business and economics. He runs meetings with his dealers and corner kids according to *Robert's Rules of Order*. He wants to expand into honest business, developing condos on the waterfront and moving past the drug trade. Prop Joe, similarly, forms a co-op for the dealers in the city. Buying into the co-op means trading a warlike mentality over territory and expansion for a mutual attitude. In exchange, you get access to the purest heroin imaginable.

Both want to ascend, moving beyond the wearisome roles that they've played as drug dealers in the world. And both, ultimately, fail disastrously. Stringer's business initiatives are perpetually stalled and foreshortened by business associates, lawyers, and politicians who want to bleed him dry of the millions of dollars of drug money he's accumulated. Prop Joe's co-op is destroyed when a young gun he brings in refuses to play by the rules.

Ultimately, both die in acts of personal betrayal. Stringer is killed when his own partner gives him up to two assassins. Prop Joe is killed by Marlo Stanfield, the young dealer he's been mentoring and trying to bring into the co-op.

Marlo, too, is denied what he ultimately wants. His meticulous methods and well-ordered team make catching him nearly impossible for McNulty and the other Baltimore cops, and his growing empire seems unstoppable once he's killed Prop Joe. But McNulty's antics get enough evidence together for a massive arrest warrant, and Marlo ends up in jail, waiting for the shoe to drop. He's unaware of what evidence they have against him and has to trust the counsel of his attorney.

But his defense lawyer is being blackmailed by the district attorney's office and is forced to essentially lie to Marlo, telling him that he can only walk away from jail if he promises to get out of the drug business forever; if he doesn't, they'll throw the book at him for the row house murders. (This, viewers know, is actually an exaggeration, a last-ditch effort by the cops to stop Marlo's reign and to end the killings.) So even as Marlo has finally assembled his empire and conquered all of his competitors, he has to walk away from it.

It's an interesting contrast with Stringer, who might have been able to live with such a deal, who seemed to want to get out of the drug game and make more money. But his downfall was preceded by being bled out (financially, that is) by real estate brokers and betrayed by his friend. In other words, he lived for money, and it never satisfied him. Marlo cared only about power and reputation. Toward the end of the show, we see him in a jail cell with members of his crew. He finds out that a competitor has been calling him out, mocking him openly, and has gone unpunished. His crew didn't tell him because they didn't want to start a war, but Marlo can't handle knowing that someone mocked him. He begins screaming at them, "My name is my *name!*" His whole life hinges upon his reputation—being feared and being dominant on Baltimore's West Side. But that too is vanity.

We last see Marlo in a suit and tie walking amongst Baltimore's high society, being introduced as a new investor. He's miserable, powerless in a room where a different kind of commerce and authority rule. He walks away, sad, shrunken a bit, and disappears into an elevator.

BETTER A LIVING DOG THAN A DEAD LION

If McNulty is the star of the show, then perhaps its soul is Omar Little (Michael K. Williams), West Baltimore's gay, shotgun-wielding, drug-stealing ("rip and run") drifter. Where most of the dealers have loyalty to a gang, Omar is a gang to himself. He haunts street corners, watching dealers and their systems for controlling drugs and money—who has the money, where is the stash kept, who is the security? When he spies a weakness, he comes in, robs them of money and drugs, and disappears. People who spot him creeping through alleys, men, women and children alike, yell warnings from open windows: "Omar's coming!" In the aftermath of his hits, he disappears, and no amount of pressure applied by his rivals can shake him loose.

In Ecclesiastes 9:4, the Teacher says that it's better to be a living dog than a dead lion. This is a remarkable phrase—dogs were the lowest of creatures in the ancient world, and lions the most noble. The Teacher, however, recognizes that there's an advantage in the living scoundrel that's not in the dead nobleman: a pulse. Omar, in many ways, embodies this advantage. His street smarts keep him alive in a world that is harsh and violent, even when he's surrounded on all sides by plenty of folks who would love to take his life.

He becomes almost an antihero. In season 2, after an innocent man gets shot for witnessing a crime, Omar is willing to testify against the gunman in court (albeit with his own motives). The defense attorney mocks the irony of a rip-and-run gunman serving as an eyewitness in a drug-related shooting, and Omar replies, "Hey, look, I ain't never put my gun on no citizen."[5]

These aren't empty words. On the streets, there's an unwritten but commonly shared set of rules that govern the way the drug trade operates. "A man gotta have a code,"[6] Omar tells Detective Bunk, and he lives by one. Omar lives and dies by this code, knowing that within the drug world, there are rules: You don't attack anyone on Sundays. You don't turn your gun on someone who isn't in the game. Punishments should be proportional to crimes. It's his way of finding meaning in a meaningless and frustrating world.

For Omar, there's no difference between blue-collar and white-collar criminals. The show often contrasts corruption in politics, police, and justice with corruption in the West Baltimore drug scene. Omar refuses to let the white-collar criminals feel immune from the stain of their sins. His strict obedience to the code of the streets gives him a sense of self-righteousness, and when he's being interrogated by an attorney, he makes his self-justification crystal clear:

Maurice "Maury" Levy (Michael Kostroff): You are amoral, are you not? You are feeding off the violence and the despair of the drug trade. You are stealing from those who themselves are stealing the lifeblood from our city. You are a parasite who leeches off . . .

    Omar: Just like you, man.

    Levy: . . . the culture of drugs. Excuse me? What?

    Omar: I got the shotgun, you got the briefcase. It's all in the game though, right?[7]

Levy freezes, and the courtroom begins to stir. He's been exposed. And Omar is exactly right. Levy is the go-to attorney for all of the big drug dealers in the city; he's happy to take their money and help them grow and protect their business. He's also happy to bleed them for every dollar he can, either through charging them a fortune or facilitating business arrangements that leave them empty—like he did to Stringer Bell. Omar sees it, understands it, and refuses to be treated as though he were any different from Levy. They are both dogs.

But like everything else in *The Wire*, Omar's obedience to the code ultimately leads to frustration. The code brings about Omar's demise. Toward the show's end, he's on a tear through West Baltimore, trying to provoke a confrontation with Marlo.

After wreaking havoc on Marlo's corners for days on end, he ends up getting shot in the head at a convenience store by a middle school kid—someone Omar would have never turned a gun on (and whose life Omar had earlier spared). The code he lived by ultimately brought about his end.

This too is meaningless.

THE END OF THE MATTER

One other character deserves mentioning, and it's his journey that provides the sole redemptive element for the show: Bubbles (Andre Royo). He's a homeless heroin addict who oscillates throughout the show between despairing and cleaning up. Through him, we see the tragedy of the drug trade. We watch him scrape together money to buy vials of heroin, we see him drooling, unconscious, on a filthy mattress in a dim room with a syringe in his veins. We see him tormented on the streets, beaten up for the little bit of money or drugs he might have. We see his sister's distrust when he tries to clean up, making him live in a padlocked basement, not even allowed to use the bathroom or travel up the stairs. His suffering, loss, and broken relationships are snapshots of the real cost of the drug trade.

After he loses a friend in a drug-related accident (which was his fault), Bubbles joins an AA-style recovery program and begins to clean up. It's not his first effort, though, and *The Wire* forces us to experience the difficulty of the rehab journey. There's no prodigal moment, an instant change of heart. There is slow progress, failure, despair, and slowly, gradually, hope.

There's a kind of redemption for Bubbles, but only after he's lost everything. Even then, it feels tenuous and uncertain.

The Wire ends with a sense of cyclical inevitability. What has happened before will happen again. A new drug boss will rise in West Baltimore. The politicians will continue their corruption. The cops will keep juking stats. The holes left by McNulty, Omar, Marlo, Prop Joe, and all the others will soon be filled again. And plenty of others will line up to buy the drugs that Bubbles has left behind.

Somehow, it doesn't *feel* like despair when you watch it. This too echoes Ecclesiastes. Throughout the book, the Teacher reminds his readers to enjoy their food and wine, to enjoy life with the one you love—because this is all we have. My friend Jonah preached a sermon on Ecclesiastes titled "Smoke 'em If You've Got 'em." It's an interesting shorthand for the book, which despairs of the vanity of life while recognizing the small pleasures in our midst.

The pleasure of *The Wire* is in the characters themselves, each of whom embody this wonderful mix of angel and demon, sinner and saint. The heroes never become two-dimensional, and even the purest amongst them, we discover, has dirt on his hands. The villains, too, stop short of being clichés. They care for mothers and girlfriends, they show loyalty to one another, they exhibit moments of compassion, and their motivations are often deeply humane. They want to matter. They want something to be proud of. They want some kind of hope beyond the despairing red bricks of the Baltimore projects they've known their whole lives.

But these aspirations disappoint them, just as the aspirations of power, greatness, and justice disappoint the cops and politicians. Only the simple pleasures are left. A shared meal in a prison. A toast in an Irish pub. A place (and a person) to come home to. These are indeed good gifts, but they can't bear the weight of humanity's deeper longings. When we ask too much of them, they crush us—just as they crush and disappoint the characters in *The Wire*.

That's the message of Ecclesiastes. Life is full of good things: love, friendship, and feasts. But these are mere goods, able to satisfy us only temporarily. A deeper and ultimately lasting satisfaction can be found only in the Giver of these gifts. If we devote our lives to attempts at finding satisfaction in these mere goods, we will end our days weary and frustrated. Thus, the Teacher ends his sermon in Ecclesiastes 12, saying: "The end of the matter; all has been heard. Fear God and keep his commandments, for this is the whole duty of man. For God will bring every deed into judgment, with every secret thing, whether good or evil" (Eccles. 12:13–14).

7

SHADOWS AND DARKNESS

We make up horrors to help us cope with the real ones.

Stephen King[1]

If you take Taylorsville Road out of Louisville, past the interstate, and out toward Taylorsville Lake, you'll find yourself in a curious, rural stretch. It's an area called Pope Lick, named after a famous salt lick nearby. Small farms and ramshackle houses dot the landscape, along with the occasional horse farm. It's gritty in places—one scary little street is piled with trash and broken-down school buses. Supposedly, there's a satanic cult compound out there. It's also the home of an infamous overland train bridge, referred to by locals as "the trestles," a seven-hundred-foot-long stretch of track that, at its tallest, stands ninety feet above the ground. The surrounding landscape is wooded and rolling hills, which masks the acoustics of the train as it approaches. The bridge is only wide enough for the train, so if you are caught out on the trestles when the train comes, you either have to jump off or be knocked off, falling to the earth below.

Every year, kids get killed on the trestle. Kids dare one another to run it between trains; when their timing is off, they get knocked off. That alone could be fodder for a scary story or two. But it's only the beginning of the story of Pope Lick.

According to the residents out there (and according to many Louisville natives), there's another reason bodies show up around the trestles. A dark presence haunts the track, feasting upon the bodies of victims when the train knocks them off. It's the Goat Man, a hideous half-man, half-goat creature, with powerful goat-like legs and fur, a human upper body, and a hybrid face with a goatlike nose and horns. He is alternatively known as the Pope Lick Monster.

I swear I'm not making this up.

One version of the legend says that long ago a circus train derailed somewhere near Floyd's Fork Creek, and the Goat Man was part of the circus's freak show. He escaped his cage when the train derailed and began wandering the hills, eating livestock and killing travelers, hobos, and passersby. When the trestles became a regular spot for teenage dares, it became his smorgasbord.

Some say he kills with an axe. Others say he throws his voice, like a siren, and lures his victims onto the trestle. Still others say he's misunderstood, and his haunting presence is meant to scare kids away from certain death when they venture out on the tracks.

Just about every city has its stories like this. Ghosts that haunt hotels. Bigfoot. El Chupacabra. Yetis. Devil Dogs. Werewolves. Vampires.

As kids, who among us didn't have a dreaded corner of the basement, closet in the house, or shadow under the bed?

Somehow we know that the shadows are hiding something. It's a suspicion the Scriptures confirm when they describe the Devil as prowling like a lion (1 Pet. 5:8), or when they reveal that our true struggle is against principalities and powers of darkness (Eph. 6:12). The book of Revelation shows us a glimpse of that dark spiritual reality, with its images of monsters, angels, and mythical beasts.

If we believe the Bible to be true, we must admit that there is more to this world than we perceive. Powers and persons that we can't see or comprehend are at work, but somehow we intuit them. That intuition works itself out in our imaginations, and we tell stories that try to explain what we feel and comfort us from fear of the shadows.

A WORLD SIMMERING WITH FEAR

Horror movies specialize in exploring our fear of what lurks in the shadows. Movies like *Paranormal Activity* (1–4), *The Exorcist, The Possession, The Devil Inside, The Last Exorcism*, and the classic *Rosemary's Baby* zero in on our fear of the supernatural. And slasher villains like Michael Myers, Freddy Krueger, and Jason have haunted silver screens for years.

These movies have an almost eschatological flavor. Some "original sin" has unleashed monsters into the world, and the end of the films usually feels like a happy-ever-after. Evil has been vanquished, and the world can rest easy. (Until the sequel, of course.)

Yet another take on the horror genre is judgment films. In the Final Destination franchise, someone has a premonition about an accident and manages to prevent it, saving many lives. But death won't be cheated, and viewers are "entertained" with the horrific and random ways each of the survivors dies. *I Know What You Did Last Summer* is another in the genre. The Scream franchise, too, played with this theme. The original killers were hunting Sydney because of the sins of her mother.

Sam Raimi launched his career with horror films. *The Evil Dead 1* and *2* introduced Raimi's style, a mix of cartoonish violence, gore, and jump-out-of-your-seat scariness. They, along with *Army of Darkness*, have become cult classics. He also directed *Spider-Man 1* and *2* (starring Tobey Maguire), but returned to horror in 2009 with *Drag Me to Hell*.

A twist on the judgment film, *Drag Me to Hell* is a morality tale about a young loan officer named Christine Brown (Alison Lohman) who has an opportunity to extend the mortgage of Sylvia Ganush (Lorna Raver)—an old Gypsy woman who has fallen behind in her payments. Christine faces a choice: she can show her grace or refuse the extension. If she refuses the extension, she will put herself in the good graces of her boss at the bank. She refuses, and invites the wrath of Sylvia upon her. As Christine leaves the bank that evening, Sylvia attacks her in the parking garage. The scene is classic Raimi— relentlessly gross, funny, violent, and over-the-top. The scene ends with Sylvia tearing a button from Christine's coat, uttering a curse, and disappearing.

With a feeling of foreboding, Christine and her skeptic boyfriend visit a fortuneteller named Rham Jas (Dileep Rao). While reading her palm, he sees that she's been cursed, and tells her that she will be tormented by a dark spirit called the Lamia. After three days, the Lamia will appear in its fullness and drag her to hell. The tormenting is both frightening and hilarious. It seems like every evil spirit is intent on throwing up on Christine—more specifically, throwing up or losing an appendage (like eyes or false teeth) in her mouth. It's truly gross. Again, it's classic Raimi.

What ensues is a series of attempts to satisfy or overcome the Lamia. First Christine kills her kitten as an attempted sacrifice, and then pays an old medium ten thousand dollars to channel the spirit into a goat, so they can kill the goat (as a literal scapegoat) and satisfy the Lamia. These attempts both fail. The Lamia mocks the death of the kitten, returning the carcass to Christine and telling her that the sacrifice won't satisfy him. As the third day approaches, Rham Jas offers one final option—she can pass the cursed object on to someone else, and when the Lamia appears, it will drag him to hell instead.

Her first choice is to pass it on to a stranger, but her conscience gets the better of her. Her second choice is a conniving coworker, but just as she gets him to foolishly accept the object, she backs out. Finally, she realizes that by digging up the Gypsy woman's body (who died the day after their conflict), she can give the object to her and send the Lamia after her soul instead. The film roars to a climax with an amazing fight against a handkerchief (again—classic Raimi) as Christine rushes to a graveyard. It's the stuff of classic Hollywood horror: at nighttime, in a rainstorm, digging up a Gypsy woman's grave to return a cursed button.

As she passes the object on to the Gypsy woman's corpse (and after more mouth-to-mouth vomiting) the rainstorm causes a flood, and Christine is buried in mud in the grave with Sylvia. Then, just as the sun rises on the third day (since the curse was pronounced), Christine's hand reaches out of the mud and climbs to safety. It's a resurrection image, and the audience feels assured that Christine is now safe.

She showers and heads to the train station, where her boyfriend awaits to whisk her off on a weekend getaway (where he plans to surprise her with an engagement ring). Christine buys a new coat at the train station and arrives on the platform having risen from the grave and wearing new robes (so to speak).

Only things aren't quite finished. Surprised by her new coat, her boyfriend reaches into his bag and produces the cursed button. There was a mix-up in his car earlier, and the envelope Christine shoved down Sylvia's corpse's throat was the wrong one (early in the film, Christine gives her boyfriend a rare coin she'd found at her bank, and it was in a similar envelope). She realizes her mistake just in time to fall on the tracks and be sucked into hell by the Lamia. The end. It's pretty stark.

In her story, Christine goes through several attempts at salvation. She makes multiple sacrifices—substitutionary acts of atonement—but they fail to satisfy the wrath of the Lamia. She tries to take on the Lamia face to face, killing it by embodying it in the goat, and fails. At the end, she attempts to pass the curse onto another, and yet again she fails. The images are blatant—she descends into a grave and is buried. She rises on the dawn of the third day, and she puts on new clothes. (If the coat had been white, it would have been perfectly biblical—but it was blue.)

But these attempts fail. Her performance was imperfect, and at the end of all her work, she remains in possession of the cursed object, and thus remains cursed. The wrath won't be satisfied with a kitten or a goat. The darkness remains bent on hunting her down.

At the root of Christine's condemnation was not some heinous sin; it was a lack of grace and mercy. *Drag Me to Hell* has some interesting parallels to a Scottish fairy tale called *The Girl and the Dead Man*. In it, three daughters are sent away from their home with the option of a small meal and a blessing or a large meal and a curse. The first two leave with the large meal and the curse. In the world, they have the opportunity to share their meals, and both refuse. They meet horrible ends in short time. The third daughter accepts the small meal and the blessing. She accepts less materially, and more spiritually. Given the opportunity to share what she has, she does, and reaps rewards for it. In the end, her wisdom and generosity lead to her ability to resurrect her sisters.

Christine needed to prove that she was tough to her bosses. She wanted to advance—she wanted more, and thus chose the "larger meal" and the curse. Had she chosen grace and sympathy over this larger meal, she would still be alive.

Stories like *Drag Me to Hell* and *The Girl and the Dead Man* show us that there are, indeed, dark forces at work in the world, and they tend to coincide with the darkness at work within each of us. The Devil indeed prowls like a roaring lion, seeking opportunity to work in concert with the evil in men's hearts.

THE TWILIGHT ZONE

Rod Serling had a name for the dark space where our inner worlds intersect with the unknown and unseen world of the mysterious and paranormal: *The Twilight Zone*. One of television's most influential shows of all time, it began with Serling's famous monologue:

> There is a fifth dimension, beyond that which is known to man. It is a dimension as vast as space and as timeless as infinity. It is the middle ground between light and shadow, between science and superstition, and it lies between the pit of man's fears and the summit of his knowledge. This is the dimension of imagination. It is an area which we call the Twilight Zone.[2]

Serling employed writers such as Charles Beaumont, Ray Bradbury, and Richard Matheson—giants of twentieth-century science fiction. The series inspired countless others, such as Chris Carter, M. Night Shyamalan, and J. J. Abrams, and is the grandfather of shows such as *The X-Files*, *Fringe*, *Lost*, *Twin Peaks*, *Amazing Stories*, *The Outer Limits*, and many, many more.

The Twilight Zone often played with concepts of perception, calling into question our finite human ability to understand our reality. In the show's first episode, a man with amnesia wanders about an abandoned town. He's wearing military fatigues and looking everywhere for signs of human life or some explanation for how he got there. Did he drop a bomb?

Is everyone dead? At an empty dime store he becomes more and more panicked as his search continues, until he begins feverishly pressing a button on a crosswalk and crying for help.

The camera cuts to a massive, empty military warehouse, where officers sit watching the man. He's inside of a five-by-five box, undergoing a test on isolation. We discover that he's been there for 484 hours and 36 minutes. He's an Air Force test subject, undergoing extreme isolation in preparation for a trip to the moon.

The whole town, all of its details, was manufactured by his mind in an attempt to handle the extreme stress of isolation. You can't trust your senses, Serling says.

The reliability of our perceptions is a theme Serling plays with a lot. One famous episode from 1963 titled "Nightmare at 20,000 Feet" features William Shatner as Bob Wilson, a passenger on a commercial air flight. In the recent past, Bob had a nervous breakdown on a plane, and he's only recently left the sanatorium. Now, he sees a monster on the wing of the plane, and no one believes him; it darts out of sight when anyone else looks toward the window. Is he hallucinating? Or is it real? Stakes grow higher as the monster begins to damage the wing, and Bob knows that unless he does something, the plane will surely crash. He steals a revolver from a policeman (it was a different era in air security, indeed), and opens the emergency exit, shooting the monster off the wing. When the plane lands, he's taken away in a straightjacket—though we're led to believe not for long. There's damage on the wing from the monster.

Here again, perceptions are called into question, but this time, the fantastic was true. There *is* something insidious out in the darkness.

My personal favorite episode is titled "The Monsters Are Due on Maple Street." It begins with a bright flashing in the sky over a serene suburban neighborhood. Suddenly, there's no electricity and all the cars stop working. People begin to question what to do next, and a child comes forward with a theory: aliens have landed. Not only that, he theorizes that they've probably placed a family in the neighborhood that looks human, but isn't—a sort of advance team. Everyone grows tense and suspicious. They debate different options for how to proceed. Behavior is questioned. A resident named Charlie (Jack Weston) grabs a shotgun and shoots an approaching shadow, which turns out to be a neighbor. Then Charlie's lights come on. Now everyone is suspicious of Charlie. Things devolve quickly, and soon there's an all-out riot. They've all become monsters, and are killing one another.

Once again the camera pans away to a nearby hillside, where two aliens are observing the chaos below. They've been manipulating the electricity, and they're both stunned at how easy it was to instill fear and fury in the humans below. There's no need to declare war on the humans; they can easily destroy themselves.

The show ends with Serling's narration:

> The tools of conquest do not necessarily come with bombs and explosions and fallout. There are weapons that are simply thoughts, attitudes, and prejudices—to be found only in the minds of men. For the record, prejudices can kill. And suspicion can destroy. And a thoughtless, frightened search for a scapegoat has a fallout all its own—for the children and the children yet unborn. And the pity of it is that these things cannot be confined to the Twilight Zone.[3]

Like in *Drag Me to Hell*, the darkness isn't just something "out there"; it's within us as well. There are terrors in the darkness, but they only need to tap into the darkness within our own hearts to accomplish their purposes.

I WANT TO BELIEVE: *THE X-FILES*

The show that haunted my dreams as a kid was *The X-Files*. It had a special blend of mystery, sci-fi, horror, and comedy. Over its nine seasons, the series followed FBI investigations into unexplained phenomena, primarily through the work of Agents Fox Mulder (David Duchovny) and Dana Scully (Gillian Anderson).

Mulder is a pariah at the FBI, obsessed with the supernatural and the existence of aliens. Scully comes to his side as the brainy skeptic, assigned with verifying (or perhaps debunking) Mulder's work. Mulder's personal history drives him. As a child, his sister was mysteriously abducted. Mulder believes that she was taken by aliens, and part of his motivation in running the X-files investigations is to get to the bottom of her disappearance.

The two agents bounce around the country, investigating strange crimes that range from serial killers to alien abductions to mythical beasts. Like *The Twilight Zone*, *The X-Files* asks many questions about perception and reality. For most of the show's run (and certainly its best seasons), one was left to wonder whether any of Mulder's theories were true. Every time evidence would emerge that seemed to verify his theories, something else would emerge to call it into question. Gradually, the show led to a state of paranoia. Was Mulder delusional, or was something else at work? Could something massive, something terrible be going on just out of sight of everyday life?

A great example of the show's paranoia and confusion is "Jose Chung's 'From Outer Space,'" from season 3. The episode opens with a typical alien abduction scene. Two teenagers are driving down a country road when their car stalls. Suddenly, white light shines in the windows, and two aliens appear. The teenagers are mysteriously knocked unconscious, and as the aliens drag them back to their ship, another ship appears.

A different species of alien appears, red and rocky with a horn on its head.

Suddenly the two kidnapping aliens look at one another and exchange surprised words. In English.

The whole episode is told as a series of recollections. Jose Chung (Charles Nelson Reilly), a bestselling author, has taken interest in the case. During the episode, he's interviewing Agent Scully and recounting the stories he's heard from various characters. All the stories conflict and overlap, and details emerge that sound absurd. Apparently aliens didn't kidnap the teenagers; the flight crew of a top-secret Air Force craft meant to look like aliens did. Their mission was interrupted by Lord Kinbote, a traveler from the earth's core.

The episode is hilarious. It includes Men in Black (mysterious nondescript strangers that explain away alien appearances) played by Jesse Ventura and Alex Trebek, and a character named Roky Crikenson (William Lucking), who journeys with Lord Kinbote to the middle of the earth, where Crikenson is given a message that will save the world. There's a comedy of errors involving hypnosis, where stories seem to erase themselves and testimony shifts.

What the episode demonstrates so well is the difficulty of describing any out-of-the-ordinary phenomenon. Everyone's story sounds ridiculous and implausible. Is everyone crazy? Or do stories change because they're embarrassing? Is the absurdity itself part of the problem?

One of the Men in Black calls out the problem plainly. "Your scientists have yet to discover how neural networks create self-consciousness, let alone how the human brain processes two-dimensional retinal images into the three-dimensional phenomenon known as perception. Yet you somehow brazenly declare that seeing is believing!"[4]

Like *The Twilight Zone*, *The X-Files* wrestles with how we know what we know. It nags the viewer with the suspicion that something more is going on—something frightful and terrible. Over time, the show's paranoia takes the shape of a massive political conspiracy involving aliens and the US government. We learn that quietly, just out of view, terrible powers are conspiring against us.

Simultaneously, the series wrestles with the doubt and skepticism that pervade modern consciences. One of the most famous episodes is "Clyde Bruckman's Final Repose." A series of murders targeting fortunetellers and palm readers brings Mulder and Scully to town. There, the local police have recruited the help of The Stupendous Yappi (Jaap Broeker) to help with the case. Yappi is a professional psychic, and Mulder is skeptical of his abilities. Yappi arrives at the scene of one crime and makes a big show of spouting some generalities, and promptly kicks Mulder out of the room, saying, "Skeptics like you make me sick."[5]

Meanwhile Clyde Bruckman (Peter Boyle) discovers a body in a dumpster. Bruckman is a local insurance agent with the psychic ability to see how people are going to die. When Mulder brings him to the crime scene, he repeats—word for word—what Yappi said.

The way the story is told, the audience knows that Bruckman's "gift" is real. By paralleling him with Yappi, we're left to wonder whether Yappi might not be real too—even if he is an attention hound.

Bruckman sees his ability as a burden, and lives his life haunted by death. Mulder tries to encourage him, calling it a gift. Bruckman says, "The only problem is that it's nonreturnable."[6] They discuss the benefits of knowing the future, and Bruckman is depressed and fatalistic.

"But if the future is written . . . why bother doing anything?" Mulder asks.

"Now you're catching on," says Bruckman.[7]

By the show's end, Bruckman has killed himself, overburdened by his constant visions of death. It leaves us to wonder whether the veil over our eyes is actually a gift.

KEEPING YOU SAFE

Part of the magic of *The X-Files* is its dual assurance. On the one hand, something terrible is happening just out of sight, but on the other, we can all go to bed and sleep well, knowing that Mulder and Scully are out there, working on our behalf to save the world.

The same could be said of any number of similar stories. *Buffy the Vampire Slayer* was about teenage vampire hunters constantly under pressure to save the world from apocalyptic attacks by the forces of evil. *Grimm* has a similar theme. Nick Burkhardt (David Giuntoli) is a Grimm, one of a long line of supernatural hunters that protect the world from all kinds of mythical creatures.

The Men in Black movies are based on similar premises. The Men in Black is a secret organization that manages earth's relationships with other planets and maintains order with the aliens who come and go from this world.

These shows offer comfort in the face of evil, telling us that powerful, heroic forces in the world are keeping us safe.

REMOVING THE MYSTERY, OR WHY THE END OF *LOST* SUCKED

The addictive power of shows about the supernatural is in their ability to sustain a sense of mystery. So long as they keep us guessing about what's actually going on, they hold us captive. *The X-Files* lost much of its addictive strength the moment we found out that the aliens were real. Mulder and Scully could continue to solve monster-of-the-week mysteries, but the bigger narrative lost its punch.

The same thing is true of *Twin Peaks*, David Lynch's fever dream of a series about the murder of a high school girl. Once the murderer was revealed, the show lost its hold on the audience. It branched out into increasingly bizarre and dark strains of storytelling, but lost its audience; the show was cancelled in the second season.

And of course, there's *Lost*, a show that hypnotized massive audiences, slowly revealing a wide array of mysterious elements involving monsters, time travel, conspiracy, murder, and alternate realities. Its final episode was almost universally anticipated and hated. Mike Hale, a critic for *The New York Times*, described it like this: "After years of insane complication of plot and character, no ending could have 'explained' the show in a wholly satisfying way, and it might have been better not to try."[8]

Once all the lights are turned on and the mysteries are explained, we lose interest in the imaginary world. The real world remains mysterious and incomprehensible. Maybe a story that clears up the mysteries and ties everything up with a bow becomes unbelievable to a world that is full of chaos.

In our dark and broken world, we rarely get easy answers. The darkness we witness—whether it's the abduction of little girls reported on the evening news, ritualistic murders carried out in our hometown, or legends about monsters in the woods devouring teenagers—is rarely "answered" in a satisfying manner. A killer might be tried and convicted, we might send "Ghost Hunters" out looking for the monsters, and we might solve the occasional mystery, but the conclusions are inevitably met by new mysteries, new horrors that happen every day. We remain in a world where the darkness continues to simmer, in cities and towns full of craven appetites and landscapes full of mystery.

We tell these stories because they resonate with our sense that there is something out there. The monster under the bed is real. The vampire does wait for us in the closet. A sinister force awaits in the shadows, licking his chops and waiting to devour us like a roaring lion.

8

REDEMPTIVE VIOLENCE

The noir hero is a knight in blood caked armor. He's
dirty and he does his best to deny the fact that he's a
hero the whole time.

Frank Miller

Of all the chapters in this book, this is the most likely to make
Christians cringe. Some of the films and TV shows I discuss are
going to be hard for many consciences, and so I want to repeat
what I said in the "Before We Begin" section: I am not necessarily recommending you watch everything I assess. Instead,
consider these (particularly *Dexter* and the Tarantino films)
to be extreme examples of a concept that appears in a variety
of ways.

So far, we've looked at two general themes: creation and
fall. When we think about creation as a theme in stories, we
see that we all long for home—whether we have a sense of
Paradise lost (Eden) or we seek to find "home" in a relationship
("Bone of my bones, flesh of my flesh.") Our creation stories
also reveal that we feel doomed by the fragility of creation and
by the awareness that our acts of creativity can unleash terror
upon the world.

We've also looked at two perspectives on the fall—we could call them the *personal* and the *impersonal*. In fall stories, we see the tragic downward trajectory of heroes, and in frustration stories, we see the broader effects of sin upon the world. Life is disappointing. Nothing works out as it seems. The things we believed would satisfy us left us feeling empty and sad. Then we looked at the ways we sense simmering darkness in the world.

From here forward, we'll look at how we react to our awareness of the impact of the fall. In the presence of fallenness and brokenness, in the face of a world that isn't the way we know (intuitively, unspokenly) it should be, how do we respond? What hope is there? How are wrongs righted? How do we respond to the inner ugliness in humanity?

THE DARK KNIGHT

Many storytellers seem to be aware that redemption comes at a violent cost. Consider Batman—particularly the version of Batman in Frank Miller's comics and in Christopher Nolan's the Dark Knight films. (These are quite different from other versions of this iconic character: the cartoonish version played by Adam West and George Clooney, or the clever and detached version played by Michael Keaton in Tim Burton's films, or the self-disciplined perfectionist portrayed [brilliantly] in Grant Morrison's comics and graphic novels.)

In the Dark Knight mythology, Bruce Wayne's tragic life is a burden. The loss of his parents opened a chasm into which he welcomed all that was violent and frightening in the world around him. The Batman persona isn't just a way of hiding Bruce Wayne from the villains he confronts; it's a way of letting out something dark and terrible that lives inside him. This Batman is both terrifying and deeply human, confounded by his own weakness and self-doubt, burdened by the way that the darkness of the world echoes inside of him. As the savior of Gotham, he doesn't shine a light; he casts a shadow. He fights the darkness by becoming it, and he suffers in the suffocating loneliness of it.

Consider the obvious contrasts: Superman, Captain America, Professor X, Spider-Man, or for that matter, James Bond, Neo (Keanu Reeves) from *The Matrix*, or the heroes of any fairy tale. These are characters whose virtue is their greatest strength. They fight with moral clarity and conviction against the powers of darkness.

Batman and others made in his mold fight from a different place. Their weakness is their greatest strength. The Incredible Hulk's rage. Jason Bourne's (Matt Damon) revulsion at being manipulated and used by the powers at Treadstone and the CIA. And of course, cable TV's most morally fraught antihero: Dexter.

BLOOD-BOUGHT REDEMPTION

Dexter Morgan's (Michael C. Hall) life is marked by two births: the physical birth when his mother brought him into the world, and the spiritual birth inside a shipping container, when Dexter was a tiny child and saw his father cut his mother to pieces with a chainsaw. It was a baptism in blood. He sat in that dark pool until rescued by a police detective who would become his adoptive father, Harry Morgan (James Remar).

The trauma wreaked havoc on Dexter's soul, and as a child, he began to exhibit sociopathic behavior, killing neighborhood animals. Harry saw where the signs were pointing, and instead of trying to curb the behavior (something both he and Dexter seemed to think was hopeless), he trained him to channel it. He taught him a code that would both keep him from doing harm to the innocent and keep him from getting caught.

CHANNEL SURFING
True Grit and the Cost of Revenge

True Grit is a classic Western about a fourteen-year-old girl's search for her father's killer. She enlists the help of US Marshal Rooster Cogburn (John Wayne in the original; Jeff Bridges in the remake) and a Texas Ranger named La Boeuf (Glen Campbell in the original; Matt Damon in the remake). The remake follows the plot of the original, but it has the clear fingerprints of the Coen Brothers (known for such films as *No Country for Old Men*, *Raising Arizona*, *Fargo*, and *O Brother, Where Art Thou?*).

The story itself fits well with the other films discussed in this chapter. It's a revenge and atonement story, serving them up with a strong dose of American religious sentiment. As my friend Ed Marcelle put it, "It opens with a Scripture and ends with a hymn and is a sermon in between." He's right. Beneath the surface of this story is a rich dialogue about justice and the problem of evil. The theme song, repeated throughout the film, is "Leaning on the Everlasting Arms," and the young protagonist, Mattie Ross (Kim Darby in the original; Hailee Steinfield in the remake), is the portrait of steadfast faith in spite of the darkness of her circumstances.

For the Coens, heroism emerges from the fringe. In *The Hudsucker Proxy*, when an evil board of executives is looking for "some jerk we can really push around," they hire Norville Barnes (Tim Robbins).[1] But the idiot from Muncie, Indiana, looking to find his way in the big city, reveals a brilliant creative mind and foils their plans. When murderous evil is unleashed in Minnesota, a slow-talking and sweet-natured pregnant woman (Frances MacDormand's Marge Gunderson) ends up unraveling the mystery and catching the criminals. It's the everyman and commoner who ends up being transcendent.

In *True Grit*, it's the worn and one-eyed marshal (who practically lives in the bottom of a whiskey barrel) who ends up showing the meaning of the phrase "true grit." So does the fourteen-year-old girl, who takes command of her own destiny, demanding and insisting on justice when every authority in the world seems to be denying it to her. La Boeuf, the Texas Ranger in shiny spurs with a bright smile, continually disappoints. Like most of the wealthy, powerful, and credentialed figures in Coen films, he's one-upped by someone well beneath his station.

It's all very Sermon on the Mount. Society's cast-offs always seem to find themselves on top when the dust settles. It's a divine reversal: the foolish things shaming the wise. The King of kings being born in a barn and raised in backwaters.

But even as Mattie Ross faces down her nemesis and defeats him, she's immediately knocked into a pit. Revenge brings a cold comfort, resulting in descent into a snake-filled darkness. Her righteous anger doesn't result in a neat and tidy ending; it leaves her scarred, poisoned, and broken.

Revenge, even petty revenge, never ends as perfectly as we'd like, with a neat and tidy moment of "I told you so" justice. Instead, like with Mattie, our pursuit of vengeance under the sun will inevitably leave us scarred both by victimization and retribution.

Dexter, then, becomes a serial killer, driven by a deep inner darkness. But instead of carrying out his crimes on random victims or feeding a monstrous fetish, he becomes a source of vigilante justice. He indulges in slow, ritualistic killings, using the skills he's developed as a forensic blood-spatter analyst to sterilize his crime scenes and erase all evidence. For victims, he seeks out criminals who have escaped the justice system due to bureaucracy, lack of witnesses willing to testify, or legal loopholes, kidnapping them, strapping them to his table, killing them, and dropping their dismembered bodies into the Atlantic Ocean. His terrible appetite becomes the means by which he rids the city of some of its very worst scum.

In the rest of his life, he tries to appear ordinary. He looks out for his sister, Deb (Jennifer Carpenter), and marries Rita Bennett (Julia Benz), a single mom with two kids. Dexter narrates the show, and as we watch, we share his inner tensions. He wishes he were normal. Watching others he says, "They make it look so easy . . . connecting with another human being. It's like no one ever told them it's the hardest thing in the world."[2] For Dexter, it is the hardest thing. He wishes he were capable of normal relationships and feelings such as love or jealousy. In some moments, he almost seems capable of becoming like everyone else, but the inner monster always comes back.

Living this dual life isn't without consequences. The tension of the show runs the highest when Dexter appears to be on the verge of being found out. He faces the potential consequences for himself, for his wife, and for his sister if his dual identity is ever discovered. In season 4, he hunts the Trinity Killer (John Lithgow), relishing the risky relationship that emerges between the two of them. Trinity, he discovers, lives an ordinary family life, hiding his inner monster behind a veneer of religion and family values. Dexter draws close to him, hoping to learn from the way this older man has skillfully hidden himself for all these decades. Trinity, in turn, discovers Dexter's secret, and begins to haunt and hunt him in return.

By the season's end, a hunt for the Trinity Killer is in full swing by the FBI and Miami police, and Dexter knows he has to take him out before the authorities catch him. He succeeds in killing him and dropping his body off like usual into the bay, only to come home and find his infant son—alive—crying in a pool of blood in the bathroom. Trinity had killed Rita before Dexter had killed Trinity, and now the cycle of violence was being repeated.

I must admit: I was traumatized by this episode's end. Better viewers than me saw it coming, but the death of Rita took me by surprise. I suppose it brought home to me the inevitability of Dexter's grim world, the inescapability of his violent fate. Rita had been a pure and innocent presence, someone who didn't have to hide anything, someone with the integrity that Dexter lacked. Her murder shattered a thread of hope that ran through the show, because she had been the link between Dexter and a normal life.

Without Rita, that hope is gone. Her death intensifies Dexter's need to kill, both to avenge the innocent like Rita and also to redeem himself from the sins of his father, a black appetite for death formed in him as a child. But it's a black hole, a bottomless pit. It won't be filled. It won't be satisfied. It will only perpetuate the darkness—no matter how many sacrifices Dexter makes.

In season 5, this need for cleansing—purging and atoning through his sacrifices—is in sharpest relief. Dexter begins the season mourning the death of his wife, and he attempts to deal with it by returning to killing. He picks a victim named Boyd Fowler (Shawn Hatosy), a municipal worker who cleans up roadkill. Boyd has a collection of barrels rotting in a pond, each one containing a young girl who has been tortured, electrocuted, and preserved in formaldehyde.

He captures Boyd and kills him in his house, discovering after the fact that Boyd has a girl trapped in his attic. Her name is Lumen Pierce (Julia Stiles), and for an unknown amount of time, she's been the victim of torture and assault from not just Boyd, but a group of five men.

Dexter rescues her, brings her back to health, and tries to help her return to a normal life. But Lumen knows his secret, and wants to join him in seeking out the rest of her captors. He eventually allows it (after she disastrously attempts it on her own), and by the season's end, they've become lovers and killed all of her tormentors, including Jordan Chase (Jonny Lee Miller)—a high-powered manipulator who has gotten to know Dexter intimately throughout the season. In their final conflict, Chase pieces together the connections between Lumen and Dexter, mocking his attempts to be a hero. "You can't save one thing to make up for another, Dexter, it's just not the way the world works."[3] Saving Lumen won't save Dexter.

And he's right. After Chase is dead and gone, it's the end of the road for Lumen. She's done killing and wants to go home, and Dexter is wrecked. Every time someone gets to really know him—to see the monster within—she leaves him. Lumen, too, is heartbroken, but knows that Dexter can't change. "It's who you are," she tells him.[4]

In one of his most human moments on the show, Dexter breaks down, and Lumen apologizes for leaving.

"Don't be sorry your darkness is gone," Dexter says. "I'll carry it for you. I'll keep it with mine."[5]

Shortly after, he's at a birthday party for Harrison, his one-year-old son. Astor (Christina Robinson), his deceased wife's teenage daughter, sits by him at one moment, asking where Lumen is. She'd met Lumen earlier in the season, when Dexter introduced her as a tenant who rented their old house. Dexter had said, vaguely, that he was helping Lumen with something, and Astor asked about it.

"Did it make you feel better? About what happened to mom?"[6]

He shudders, and remains silent. He's killed five people with Lumen. He's witnessed a depth of horror that most of us can't imagine. He's known and been known by someone, and she's left him alone once again. Astor, who's begun to sympathize with Dexter, puts a hand on his back.

He narrates as he walks over to Harrison, picking him up to blow out his candle, thinking about Lumen. "While she was here she made me think, even for the briefest moment that I might be human. But wishes, of course, are for children."[7]

Dexter's duty, then, is to continue the bloodshed, a Sisyphean effort to stem the tide of darkness within, and a distorted echo of the book of Hebrews, which says that no amount of blood from bulls and goats—no abundance of imperfect offerings—can erase our sins (Heb. 10:4).

Like Dexter, many stories begin with a sense of "original sin"—some heinous crime that needs to be judged, punished, or avenged. In our stories we wonder, just as we do in ordinary life, if vengeance will be satisfying. For Dexter, it ultimately isn't.

VENGEANCE, JUDGMENT, AND THE DIVINE IN QUENTIN TARANTINO FILMS

One filmmaker who has made vengeance his primary motif is Quentin Tarantino. *Pulp Fiction*, his iconic 1994 film, traces redemptive violence in the lives of a handful of criminals, thugs, and lowlifes in LA. It's told in a cyclical, nonlinear format, underscoring the redemptive arcs of several characters.

After an opening scene in a diner, where Honey Bunny

(Amanda Plummer) and Pumpkin (Tim Roth) decide to rob the place, the film jumps to a different story line. We meet Vincent (John Travolta) and Jules (Samuel L. Jackson), who are muscle for Marsellus Wallace (Ving Rhames). They're on a job for Wallace, the details of which are initially unclear. After a typically Tarantino dialogue about cheeseburgers and foot massages (Tarantino is the master of funny, aimless background banter), Jules says, "Come on, let's get into character."[8]

An apartment door unlocks and opens in front of them, and they walk inside, where three young men sit. The apartment is in disarray, and its inhabitants appear shocked to see Jules and Vincent. (It's a reasonable assumption that they've been hiding out there, as we soon discover.) Jules introduces himself and Vincent as associates of Marsellus Wallace, and in the ensuing conversation we discover that these men have somehow broken trust with Wallace. Vincent recovers a briefcase hidden in the cupboard; its locks open with the combination 666. When opened, it emits an amber glow, and the audience never sees inside.

Tarantino fans have longed speculated about the briefcase's contents. Some theorize a connection to Tarantino's previous film, *Reservoir Dogs*, and wonder if it might contain diamonds or the infamous ear. Others see a spiritual meaning to the briefcase and the wrath of Wallace, wondering if somehow these men have stolen his soul. In this reading of the film, Jules and Vincent are redeeming Wallace, rescuing his soul from those who stole it and bringing wrathful vengeance with them. When we meet Wallace a little later, we see a BAND-AID at the base of his skull, and the theory goes that this is the wound from which the soul was taken.

While Tarantino has remained cryptic on the question, the story seems to support a spiritual reading of the briefcase's contents. Jules and Vincent are (echoing the Blues Brothers, whom they resemble with their black suits and skinny ties) on a mission from God, seeking justice and vengeance for Wallace. Just before killing one of the men who stole the briefcase, Jules recites Ezekiel 25:17 (not the actual verse—a hodgepodge of biblical-sounding phrases that serve the film's narrative):

> The path of the righteous man is beset on all sides by the inequities of the selfish and the tyranny of evil men. Blessed is he who, in the name of charity and good will, shepherds the weak through the valley of darkness, for he is truly his brother's keeper and the finder of lost children.[9]

Perhaps Jules and Vincent are such shepherds, rescuing Wallace's soul from his captors. Jules continues:

> And I will strike down upon thee with great vengeance and furious anger those who would attempt to poison and destroy My brothers. And you will know My name is the Lord when I lay My vengeance upon thee.[10]

Immediately after these words, Jules and Vincent unload their guns. We flash forward to a scene where Marsellus is paying Butch Coolidge (Bruce Willis) to throw a fight. Butch is an aging boxer, and Wallace tells him this is his only way to "make it" now. He's too old to keep hoping for success in the ring. Jules and Vincent arrive at the bar to deliver the briefcase, and Butch and Vincent exchange tense words (for no apparent reason).

Butch Coolidge's story actually begins (in terms of chronology) with the childhood memory of receiving a gold watch, his "birthright," as young Butch is told by Captain Koons (Christopher Walken). The watch is a family heirloom and was worn by his great-grandfather in World War I, his grandfather in World War II, and his father in Vietnam. This memory tells us that Butch comes from a long line of warriors, and the watch comes to him as part of that legacy and as testimony to the bonds of friendship that emerge in the midst of terrible suffering.

At the boxing match, Butch not only fails to throw the fight, he kills his opponent in the ring. It was his plan all along—to take the money from Wallace, win the fight anyway, and go out on the lam. He goes to a crummy motel to meet his wife. They've abandoned their home and prepared to go on the run, but as he discovers the next morning, she forgot to pack his gold watch. He must risk everything to go back to the house and get it. When he arrives, he finds Vincent waiting for him and kills him. Soon afterward, he encounters Wallace. Wallace is all wrath and the two battle it out in the streets, eventually collapsing on the floor of a pawnshop. When they awaken, they discover they've been taken captive by two men with twisted sexual appetites, who intend to make them their sex slaves. Wallace is taken away for abuse, and Butch manages to break free, but on the way out of the pawnshop he stops, unwilling to leave Wallace behind.

This is a crucial turning point for Butch. One must assume it's linked with his father's history in the Hanoi prison, where he bonded with Captain Koons. (In the flashback, Koons actually insists that if things were different, Butch's father would be talking with Koons's son.) His legacy is one of honor, brotherhood, and battle. So just as he can't throw a fight and lose on purpose, he can't abandon Wallace to the torturers. After all, Wallace's anger at Butch is justified; he took the money to throw the fight.

Butch wanders the store briefly, looking for something with which he can assault the captors, settling eventually on a samurai sword (some superfans think this might be a famous sword mentioned in *Kill Bill*, another Tarantino film). Then he descends the stairs into the hell of the torture rooms below the pawnshop. Soon one of the kidnappers is dead and the other is wounded, and Wallace and Butch come to an understanding. Because of Butch's mercy—his rescue of Wallace—he's forgiven his debts and sent away.

Here redemption is purgative. Butch earns his forgiveness after an act of compassion: descending into hell to release the captive. Note, too, that this is the second time that Wallace has been rescued by the violence of others. After coming to their understanding, Butch leaves, stealing one of the captors' motorcycles. It is emblazoned with the word *grace* on the side. He rides off, free from the wrath of Wallace and the burden of guilt over double-crossing him.

Later, we return to the earlier scene in the apartment with Jules and Vincent, where we discover another man, hidden in the bathroom with a gun, and we hear Jules quoting the Bible passage. As the gunfire ends, the man in the bathroom bursts out and unloads the pistol at Jules and Vincent, mysteriously missing them entirely.

After they kill the shooter, Jules looks around, amazed. He chalks it up to divine intervention and insists that God himself came down from heaven and stopped the bullets. Driving away, he announces his retirement. He's going to tell Wallace himself when they get back to him—he's done. This act of preservation was some kind of message from God.

After another series of events that are both violent and comical, Jules and Vincent end up at a diner eating breakfast. Their conversation turns back to the day's events, when Vincent asks Jules why he's been sitting there "all serious."

> Jules: Man, I just been sittin' here thinking.
> Vincent: 'Bout what?
> Jules: 'Bout the miracle we witnessed.
> Vincent: Miracle you witnessed. I witnessed a freak occurrence.
> Jules: What is a miracle, Vincent?

CHANNEL SURFING
Grace and Radical Acceptance

This chapter looks at vengeance and atonement as a motif for redemption. Another way to understand the gospel is as radical, scandalous grace. God, who is holy, pure, perfect, and powerful, has rescued sinners who are conniving, vicious, and "only evil continually" (Gen. 6:5). The book of Hosea depicts this metaphorically through the marriage of Hosea (the prophet) to Gomer (the whore).

In film, this kind of radical grace has been pictured many times. *Pretty Woman*, the Richard Gere/Julia Roberts romantic comedy that made Roberts's career, is about a wealthy man falling in love with a prostitute and the radical acceptance that love created. Two Paul Thomas Anderson films also demonstrate radical acceptance. *Magnolia* weaves together several stories, exploring the legacy of brokenness that is passed down generationally. As relationships collapse under the weight of sin and suffering, a storm of frogs hits Los Angeles, like the judgment on Egypt in the book of Exodus. This storm is a catalyst for a miracle; the judgment upon them all releases them and we see the possibility of healing. *Punch Drunk Love* is a much simpler story, starring Adam Sandler as Barry, a socially awkward man with a terrible rage problem. He meets Lena (Emily Watson) and falls in love almost immediately. Lena, knowing that Barry's life is a mess, accepts him anyway, and after Barry reconciles some loose ends in his life, the two seem destined for a happy-ever-after ending.

Perhaps my favorite example of radical grace in a movie is *The Mission*, starring Robert De Niro and Jeremy Irons. Irons is Father Gabriel, a Jesuit priest running a mission that reaches out to the natives. Gabriel moves to the community after the natives have taken his predecessor, tied him to a cross, and sent him over a waterfall to die. DeNiro plays Rodrigo Mendoza, a mercenary and slave trader in Central America, making his living kidnapping and selling natives to local Spanish plantations. Mendoza finds his fiancée in bed with another man, and kills him in a duel. Gabriel visits him in the aftermath, while Mendoza is spiraling into a depression. Mendoza ends up following Gabriel into the jungles, hoping to earn his salvation, carrying a massive, heavy bundle with his armor in it.

In a beautiful and moving scene, Mendoza arrives at a village from which he'd kidnapped and sold natives. Seeing his repentance and humiliation, the natives come forward and cut the bundle off his back, sending it tumbling into a ravine. It's a beautiful image of grace; the burden of his past, the burden of his shame, is cut away in an instant.

Nothing to earn, nothing to prove. Welcomed just as we are: that's the glory of grace.

Vincent: Act of God.

Jules: And what is an act of God?

Vincent: When, um, God makes the impossible possible. (Pauses) But, this morning, I don't think, qualifies.

Jules: Hey Vincent, don't you see, that @#$% don't matter. You're judging this @#$% the wrong way. I mean, it could be that God stopped the bullets, or he changed Coke to Pepsi, he found my @#$% car keys. You don't judge this @#$% on merit. Now whether or not what we experienced was an according-to-Hoyle miracle is insignificant, but what is significant is I felt the touch of God. God got involved.

>Vincent: But why?
>
>Jules: Well that's what's @#$% with me, I don't know why. But I can't go back to sleep.
>
>Vincent: You're serious? You're really thinking about quitting?
>
>Jules: The life?
>
>Vincent: Yeah.
>
>Jules: Most definitely.

Jules then announces his plan to walk the earth like Cain, wandering the earth until God puts him wherever he wants him.

>Vincent: Jules, look, what happened this morning, man, I agree, it was peculiar, but water into wine . . .
>
>Jules: All shapes and sizes, Vincent.
>
>Vincent: Don't @#$% talk to me that way, man.
>
>Jules: If my answers frighten you, Vincent, then you should cease asking scary questions.[11]

Vincent leaves for the bathroom, and we discover quickly that this is the scene of the robbery that took place in the film's opening sequence. A standoff occurs between Jules and Pumpkin when Jules refuses to hand over Marsellus Wallace's briefcase. The tensions ratchet up, and finally, Jules opens it for Pumpkin, who is enraptured when he sees its mysterious glowing contents. Jules seizes the moment to disarm him, and now the standoff is between Jules—with a gun trained upon Pumpkin (he starts calling him Ringo)—and Honey Bunny, who is spastically screaming and pointing her gun all over the place. (Vincent is still in the bathroom, reading.)

The Jules we meet in the film's opening sequence would

have quickly killed Pumpkin and Honey Bunny, but this is a changed man. This is a man who's seen too much death for one day, who's been spared of his own death by divine intervention. A man ready to go roam the earth and listen for the voice of God.

Jules asks for his wallet back, and then allows Pumpkin to take $1,500 out of it, saying it's his to keep if he'll just walk away. Everyone is confused (including Vincent, who has emerged from the bathroom and now stands with a gun pointed at Honey Bunny).

Jules recites the Bible passage again (the third time we've heard it in the film), and offers his interpretation of the passage. It used to just be something he'd say to scare people before he shot them. But now he's trying to find his place in it, to discern which part of the passage is him.

> See, now I'm thinking: maybe it means you're the evil man. And I'm the righteous man. And Mr. 9mm here . . . he's the shepherd protecting my righteous @#$% in the valley of darkness. Or it could mean you're the righteous man and I'm the shepherd and it's the world that's evil and selfish. And I'd like that. But that @#$% ain't the truth. The truth is you're the weak. And I'm the tyranny of evil men. But I'm tryin', Ringo. I'm tryin' real hard to be the shepherd.[12]

Volumes have been written about this movie and its interesting spiritual undertones. While it might seem odd to single out this nearly twenty-year-old film in this chapter, I think it's worth considering for a couple of reasons. First, Tarantino's work is derivative (in the best use of the word) of many Hollywood styles: Kung Fu, Blaxploitation, Spaghetti Westerns, '40s' and '50s' serials, Film Noir, and more. These genres are morally unambiguous, usually marked out by clear heroes and villains, good guys and bad guys. *Pulp Fiction* seamlessly dips into these various styles, weaving them together in a way that is distinctive of Tarantino's style.

To appreciate his work, you have to understand that Tarantino is a guy who loves movies and stories, and wants to have fun with the audience. His work is interactive, provoking the imagination and begging to be thought about and talked about. Tarantino seems like the kind of guy who wants to watch a movie and then go to a diner with his friends and talk about it all night. Thus, *Pulp Fiction*'s meandering, disjointed, and over-the-top style has to be seen as an effort to provoke and invite that kind of conversation. He's a show-off in the best sense, invoking the golly-gee-wow sensibilities of old Hollywood. Those old movies had a revelatory quality, inadvertently exposing much about human nature that Tarantino wants to enhance and amplify in his own work—all of which is driven by a sense of cosmic morality—justice, revenge, judgment, and resurrection.

Pulp Fiction articulates an understanding of redemption that comes only through violence. Wallace's lost briefcase—whatever it contains—returns only when wrath is poured out. Given the movie's overt spiritual elements (especially in the final, climactic scene with Jules and Pumpkin/Ringo), I think it's a good reading of the film to assume that the briefcase contains Wallace's soul, or his salvation. Whatever it contains, it is only restored after judgment and violence.

The stark violence of these scenes, their chaos and darkness, is a statement about the darkness of humanity and an accurate reflection of a biblical worldview that calls the thoughts of men "only evil all the time" (Gen. 6:5 NIV). Redemption comes at a grisly, bloody price.

Jules and Vincent, then, are witnesses to this violence. When they're miraculously untouched by the gunshots from the guy in the bathroom, they are differentiated—Vincent the skeptic and Jules the true believer.

Chronologically, we know what happens next. Jules and Vincent argue over the validity of the "miracle" they witnessed. Next, Jules refuses to kill Pumpkin and Honey Bunny, choosing not only to let them live, but even to give them the substantial cash in his wallet. We're to believe he's truly a changed man. His own vision for his future—wandering the earth and listening for the voice of God—is that of a prophet. And to Vincent's detriment, he refuses to listen to the prophet's voice.

From the diner, they go to see Wallace, who is paying off Butch to throw the fight. After he pays him, Butch and Vincent have words at the bar, and Butch goes on his way. That night, Vincent takes Mrs. Wallace out for dinner and has to give her an adrenaline shot to save her life. Sometime later (a day or two), he goes to Butch's apartment with Wallace to wait for Butch and kill him. There, Butch surprises him by coming out of the bathroom and shooting him with his own gun.

Vincent's death is the product of his unbelief. If he'd believed Jules, that God had spared them and spoken to them, he wouldn't have been in that apartment. He missed yet another lesson when Mrs. Wallace almost died. As a hit man, he came to see human life as a commodity, something to be thought of transactionally. Mrs. Wallace needed sparing only because of the wrath of Wallace. Vincent didn't learn and he didn't change. That view of life came back to bite him in Butch's apartment. I think it's no small symbolism that he died as a result of being shot with his own gun.

As I said earlier, I think *Pulp Fiction* is prototypical of all of Tarantino's films. They have a strong moral thread that unites all of them: sin, judgment, wrath, and resurrection. *Kill Bill*, starring Uma Thurman as "The Bride," is a classic revenge flick. The Bride was a member of an elite assassination squad, but she decided to retire when she found out she was pregnant. She moves to Texas, finds a nice young man, and settles down. But on her wedding day, Bill—the assassination squad's leader and her former lover—shows up to kill everyone, including the groom. The Bride wakes up from a coma in a hospital four years later, vowing revenge. In the two films, she hunts down the old squad, killing everyone in her path. She is the embodiment of wrath and judgment, a relentless superhuman force that cannot be stopped.

Inglourious Basterds is another story of wrath and judgment. It's a reimagined end to World War II. The Basterds, led by Lt. Aldo Raine (Brad Pitt), are a vicious, semirogue squadron of soldiers assigned with the task of terrorizing the Nazis in occupied France. They specialize in torture and scalping. They are assigned with an assassination job at a French movie theater, where a Nazi propaganda film is going to play for a group of Nazi heads of state. Their plot is suspected by Col. Hans Landa (Christoph Waltz), a brilliant and cold-blooded SS officer. Meanwhile, the theater owner, Shoshanna (Mélanie Laurent), a Jewish survivor, is plotting her own attack on the Nazis in her theater house.

Landa uncovers the plot and captures Raine, threatening to end the mission and have all of Raine's men killed. But he also recognizes that the war will inevitably end with the Germans losing, so if he makes a deal now, he can get favorable terms for himself. Raine reluctantly arranges to take Landa into custody, and the plan moves forward. The Basterds attack the cinema just as Shoshanna plays a film reel that announces her judgment on the Nazis. The theater bursts into flame and the Basterds start spraying bullets on the crowd of Nazi officers, socialites, and politicians—including Goebbels and Hitler himself. The whole theater ends up engulfed in flames, and the Nazi war machine has effectively had its head cut off.

Raine takes Landa to the border, where Landa expects to be treated like a war hero. Raine shoots Landa's junior officer and carves a swastika into Landa's head with a bowie knife. (He knows Landa will take the SS uniform off; he wants to make sure Landa has something that he couldn't remove.)

The movie seems to say, "Gee whiz, wouldn't it have been great if it happened like this?"[13] Tarantino offers us a vision of the war's end that is, in many ways, more satisfying. It offers a judgment that is immediate, visible, and terrible upon the monsters of the twentieth century.

And while Christians have confidence in an ultimate judgment, the hunger for that judgment—experienced at times as a desire for revenge and punishment of notorious evildoers—is an affirmation of the *goodness* of judgment. Tarantino echoes the Bible again, albeit in a way that is directed outward. We all want judgment for the world. We're more hesitant about judgment for our hearts.

The last of Tarantino's films I'll mention is *Django Unchained*. In this film a bounty hunter (Christoph Waltz, again) enlists a slave named Django (Jamie Foxx) to help find a group of fugitives. In exchange, he agrees to help Django find and purchase his wife, who has been sold at a slave auction. Where *Kill Bill* is about The Bride's wrath against her husband's killers and *Inglourious Basterds* is about God's (or humanity's or fate's, depending on how you read it) wrath against the Nazi regime, *Django Unchained* is about wrath against the institution of slavery, which Tarantino forces his audience to behold. We see a slave woman lashed with a whip, a man torn apart by dogs, and Django stripped and hung upside down, threatened with castration. Django has an otherworldly fury and aim with his pistol, and the movie is one of Tarantino's bloodiest.

Whenever we see crime and wrongdoing, we want someone to pay. We want to see the cost accounted for, and we want to know that this evil is vanquished from the earth. Tarantino offers that in his movies, and he ends his movies—especially *Inglourious Basterds* and *Django Unchained*—with a knowing wink at the audience. Stories are often criticized for ending a little too neatly or a little too tidily, but Tarantino relishes in that kind of ending in these two films. I think that's why *Pulp Fiction* doesn't end with Butch's story (which is chronologically last); Tarantino wants to end with the spiritual lift of a life changed, a world better, and an evil conquered, even if that evil is only inside Jules's heart.

Only Hollywood can offer us stories where the end feels complete, where things are tied up in a bow. Often, these kinds of stories feel thin and flimsy; it's the brilliance of Tarantino and his over-the-top style that enables his stories to transcend the corny, pulpy films that inspired him.

It's the happy ending we all hunger for, and it's something this world too often denies. Juries get verdicts wrong. Criminals and despots kill themselves before they can face trial. Even when we get the bad guy in real life, the results are still unsatisfying. But it's precisely because of such dissatisfaction that stories like *Django* exist. They offer a clear answer that our hearts ache for in ordinary life.

But we're not a people without hope in this area. There is another who will come one day, descending from the clouds, wielding a sword, freeing the world from its captors once and for all. Until that day, all we can say is, "Come, Lord Jesus."

9

HEROES AND MESSIAHS

Before it was a Bomb, the Bomb was an Idea. Superman, however, was a Faster, Stronger, Better Idea.

Grant Morrison, *Supergods*

It's July 22, 2013, and throughout this entire day, on the news and in social media, there's been a steady buzz of anticipation. Kate is in labor. Not just any Kate—Catherine, Dutchess of Cambridge, wife of Prince William, heir to the throne of the United Kingdom.

It's remarkable the way the British monarchy captures and thrills American imaginations (like mine). In the 1980s, it was Charles and Diana's fairy-tale wedding that caught our attention, as did Diana's humanitarianism and celebrity. That interest was only magnified by our voyeuristic fascination with their divorce and Diana's tragic death. William and Kate seem to have captured a similar ethos. There is something hopeful about a king, something that we just can't help but pay attention to.

History would caution us otherwise. Far too often, our enthroned kings have been tyrants and despots. In modern times, the title of *king* has been eschewed and replaced with new terms—chancellor, president, supreme leader—but the concept of a leader with absolute authority has hardly faded from the world's political scene. We know these men by name far more than by title: Hitler, Lenin, Stalin, Pol Pot, Castro, Kim Jong-il, and many more.

As much as these figures have made their mark and left their stain on world history, we remain transfixed by the idea of the good king: a leader that could unite us and bring peace. It fills our stories, our epic poems and comic books, our summer blockbusters and December Oscar-seekers. It's an ethos that politicians of all stripes want to capture, and in the United States, perhaps no one in my lifetime has done so more powerfully than Barack Obama in his 2008 "Hope" campaign. Everywhere you looked—on T-shirts and bumper stickers and yard signs and lapel buttons—you saw the images and icons of that campaign, a dreamy and muted red, white, and blue depiction of Obama's name, first initial, or face, staring off in the distance with the austerity of our national icons.

Obama has proven as human as any other leader, burdened by filibusters, gridlock, and the complexity of our national security issues. His failures might leave some slower to anoint their next candidate with such high expectations, but we can be sure that it won't be the last time a candidate seizes idealistic hopes to win an election. The part of us looking for a hero remains, ready to be tapped by the next politician, preacher, or action star who appears ready to take on the evils of the world.

It's a hunger that fills in the gaps of our histories, as well. Heroism gets attached to the gauzy memories we have of previous heads of state like Lincoln, Washington, or Adams, or more recently, Reagan or Kennedy. And on a more personal level, many of us gloss over our memories of parents and grandparents in the same way. We remember their triumphs in a way that outshines their failures.

And of course, this is far from a modern phenomenon.

GIVE US A KING

In 1 Samuel 8, the people of Israel ask God for a human king. It's a strange request, given their history. They have inherited an amazing legacy: God himself rescued them from their chains in Egypt, demonstrating incomprehensible power through the plagues—not to mention parting the Red Sea. He's led them through the wilderness to their homeland, and he's conquered their enemies and kept them safe, when they've kept their end of the covenant.

But they look with envy upon their neighbors and the human kings that rule them. Something about the concept of a human king appeals to them, and so they continue their pleading.

Samuel warns them:

> "These will be the ways of the king who will reign over you: he will take your sons and appoint them to his chariots and to be his horsemen and to run before his chariots. And he will appoint for himself commanders of thousands and commanders of fifties, and some to plow his ground and to reap his harvest, and to make his implements of war and the equipment of his chariots. He will take your daughters to be perfumers and cooks and bakers. He will take the best of your fields and vineyards and olive orchards and give them to his servants. He will take the tenth of your grain and of your vineyards and give it to his officers and to his servants. He will take your male servants and female servants and the best of your young men and your donkeys, and put them to his work. He will take the tenth of your flocks, and you shall be his slaves. And in that day you will cry out because of your king, whom you have chosen for yourselves, but the LORD will not answer you in that day."

But the people refused to obey the voice of Samuel. And they said, "No! But there shall be a king over us, that we also may be like all the nations, and that our king may judge us and go out before us and fight our battles." (1 Sam. 8:11–20)

The story that unfolds in 1 Samuel—the kingship of Saul and David—illuminates much about the consequences and limits of human heroes. Saul takes the throne with great potential, but his hubris and his love of the attention of his people keeps him from being a great leader. His downfall is painful and tragic. David arises as a slayer of giants, a great warrior, thinker, and poet, who wins the hearts of the people while he himself seeks hard after the face of God. But this hero, too, is flawed. He commits adultery and murder, and is ashamed of it. His sons bicker over his throne, and the peace he establishes fades within a generation.

In spite of all of this, the hunger for a hero continues to burn in Israel. The Psalms and Prophets are full of imagery of David's throne, building on the nation's legacy with a weighty hope for the future. The hope that led the people to cry out for a human king in the first place continued unabated, even as their kings and leaders disappointed. It's as though the desire for such a hero were written on the human heart.

HISTORY AND HEROES

Throughout history, imaginations have run wild with hero hunger. Literature and mythology are full of it, passing on tales of men like Odysseus, Hercules, Beowulf, and King Arthur (to name just a few) who took on superhuman tasks in order to save humanity or to prove their mettle.

The parallels between these stories are often striking. Joseph Campbell, building on the work of psychologist Carl Jung, described that parallelism with a twelve-stage framework called "The Hero's Journey." It's amazing how many hero stories—from Luke Skywalker to James Bond to Jesus—fit within Campbell's framework.

For Jung and Campbell, this journey is as much about self-discovery and self-actualization as it is about the heroics of any particular story. The hero's journey is transformative. He or she moves from self-centeredness to others-centeredness. They are wiser, and their presence is a gift to the world.

For Campbell, Jesus is one myth among many. But as a Christian, I have to wonder what came first. Did the Jesus "myth" emerge for the same reasons as Odysseus or Spider-Man? Or did these other myths emerge because the hunger for the Hero is written in our hearts?

In Genesis 3, when sin enters the world, it comes with a promise. Eve's offspring will face off with the Serpent again, and while the Serpent will strike his heel, he will crush the Serpent's head (Gen. 3:15). From the moment we were cast from the garden to the wilderness, we were on the lookout for the Hero.

If our lives and our stories are really encapsulated in this greater story—of creation, fall, redemption, and consummation—then just as we grapple with our fallenness and invent stories that parallel the truth, it would make sense that our stories both intentionally and unintentionally resonate with the coming of the Messiah.

So in the spirit of Campbell, let's consider the hero's journey with Jesus as the archetypical hero, and consider the way other heroic journeys echo his.

THE JOURNEY OF JESUS

Called Away: The Incarnation

Jesus's journey begins in the throne room. Possessing all of the glory of the godhead, he made the decision to humble himself:

> Though he was in the form of God, [he] did not count equality with God a thing to be grasped, but emptied himself, by taking the form of a servant, being born in the likeness of men. (Phil. 2:6–7)

From the glory of the throne room, he descended to the womb of a young girl and was born in a stable. St. Jerome, speaking in a homily from around the fourth century, described it like this:

> He found no room in the Holy of Holies that shone with gold, precious stones, pure silk, and silver. He is born not in the midst of gold and riches, but in the midst of dung, in a stable (wherever there is a stable, there is also dung) where our sins were more filthy than the dung. He is born on a dunghill in order to lift up those who come from it; "from a dunghill he lifts up the poor" (Ps. 113:7).[1]

At the beginning of Jesus's journey, he has to answer a calling. Sent by the Father, he chooses to forsake the comforts of glory for the sake of others. He must leave home.

Tried and Tested: The Temptations of Jesus

In his life, Jesus faced every temptation, like us, yet was without sin (Heb. 4:15). We can believe that the ordinary, everyday sins we struggle against were struggles for Jesus, too. He was tempted with pride, lust, greed, gluttony, and self-centeredness, just as we are. He faced persecution and distrust from his family and friends and from the religious authorities. He journeyed to the desert to face temptation from the Devil himself. Yet he did not sin.

These trials weren't merely external; they were about his true identity. Could he remain faithful to his mission in spite of the external pressures? Could he remain faithful to God's Word while under terrible fatigue and stress? Satan, knowing who Jesus was, confronted his physical weakness (telling him to turn stones to bread), questioned his heavenly calling (daring him to leap from the tower), and challenged his loyalty to the Father (enticing Christ to worship him, the Devil). Satan attacked Jesus's true identity.

Likewise, during his ministry, Jesus was constantly pressured to back down from his radical theological statements, and his family seemed embarrassed by him. He must have had a certainty about who he was and what he was called to.

His greatest internal challenge had to be at Gethsemane. Far worse than the constraints of his humanity or the scorn of his critics and doubters, he was preparing to face the wrath of God. He wanted his friends to watch and pray with him, but they didn't, and he faced the challenges alone, praying, weeping, sweating blood, and asking God to "let this cup pass" from him (Matt. 26:39).

In the end, Jesus prayed, "Not my will, but yours" (Luke 22:42), and he continued the journey.

Into the Darkness: The Crucifixion

Soon, Jesus takes the journey into the clutches of the Romans. He is stripped, beaten, tried, convicted, and paraded through town to Golgotha, a hill outside the city where he's crucified. The sky turns black, he breathes his last, and the earth quakes. Dead people walk out of their tombs. The temple curtain tears.

In ways that we can't quite comprehend, Jesus has won the battle. He's conquered Satan, sin, and death, not with a direct battle, but with an act of self-sacrifice. In his ultimate humility, he's accomplished ultimate victory. The Apostles' Creed states that Jesus "descended into hell"—a statement worth some theological debate, but also worth considering as a poetic reference. What we know for certain is that he who knew no sin *became* sin for us (2 Cor. 5:21). He descended into the darkness for the sake of those he loved.

Out of the Darkness: The Resurrection

For three days, Jesus's body lay in a borrowed tomb. It seemed to the watching world that the battle was lost, that Jesus had failed in his mission. But on the morning of the third day, two women went to the tomb, intending to anoint his body for burial, and found the greatest surprise in history. The tomb was empty. Jesus was alive.

This is the culmination of Jesus's work. The miracles, the reinterpretation of the law, the confounding of the Pharisees, and the compassion for the down-and-out—all of it was a foretaste, a preview, of this magnificent work. In the resurrection, God's promises for the restoration of all things find their assured "amen." As N. T. Wright put it: "The resurrection completes the inauguration of God's kingdom. . . . It is the decisive event demonstrating that God's kingdom really has been launched on earth as it is in heaven."[2]

It's Jesus's victory moment. Throughout his life, he's announced that the kingdom of God is "at hand." In the cross, he's proven the kingdom's power. Death has been encountered and conquered. We too will one day, once and for all, be free from its tyranny (1 Cor. 15:26). The cross that was an instrument of suffering and shame becomes a banner of victory for all who trust in Jesus.

Home Again: The Ascension

Crucial to the journey of Jesus is the ascension. The Son, sent by the Father to carry out his mission on earth, returns to the throne room, victorious. His work continues, but it's not the work of war and struggle. It is the work of *presence* (Hebrews 8). From his place beside the Father, Jesus the God-

Man intercedes on our behalf, making us present to God and God present to us. The cross guarantees our access to God now, just as it guarantees our hope for the future.

Taken as a whole, Jesus's life and journey can be marked by five stages:

- *Called Away*. He was called away from the throne room and into the humbling form of a child.
- *Tried and Tested*. His journey's ultimate goal was the cross, but on the way, he faced challenges to his calling and identity. These challenges had to be overcome in order for him to complete his mission.
- *Into the Darkness*. At the cross, Jesus faced his greatest test, enduring pain, shame, and the ultimate darkness of God's wrath.
- *Out of the Darkness*. At the resurrection, Jesus emerged victorious from his greatest test.
- *Home Again*. Jesus returned to the Father, now able to carry out a greater ministry.

This journey (which, again, is similar to Jung and Campbell's "Hero's Journey") is repeated again and again in the stories we tell. Let's consider just a few of them.

THE JOURNEY OF FRODO

Frodo Baggins of J. R. R. Tolkein's Lord of the Rings trilogy is an iconic hero of literature and film.

His journey begins in the Shire, a place that's nearly utopian. Hobbits live quiet lives, enjoying good food, friendship, songs, and parties. Frodo's Uncle Bilbo decides to retire to the mountains and live out his last days, and he leaves his estate to Frodo. Soon, the wizard Gandalf becomes suspicious about one of Frodo's heirlooms: a golden ring that makes its wearer invisible. He discovers that it's the Ring of Power, belonging to Sauron, an evil sorcerer who once dominated Middle Earth. Sauron is amassing power and armies, preparing for another war, and the only hope of defeating him is in destroying the ring.

Frodo's calling, then, is away from the Shire, away from the comforts of home and family, to carry the ring to Mount Doom in the land of Mordor, where fires burn hot enough to destroy the ring forever.

The ring plagues its keeper with an infectious and hateful presence. Frodo is tried and tested by carrying the ring. He's hunted by Sauron's armies and pressured by evil men to give the ring away, so they might use it for their own ends.

Carrying the ring diminishes Frodo, and his transformation of mood and form follows the path of Smeagol, another Hobbit who once possessed the ring (or perhaps, was possessed *by* the ring). The ring unnaturally extended Smeagol's life, wilting him into Gollum, a grey, withering shadow of his previous form. Gollum stalks Frodo, eager to steal the ring back. At times, he becomes an ally, but more often, he reveals himself to be deceitful and scheming. Frodo bears this burden, too, all while journeying through a brutal landscape.

Frodo's journey into darkness is his ascent up Mount Doom. There, he faces his greatest test: can he destroy the ring, or has it taken too great of a possession of him?

Throughout the books (and movies), Gandalf has foreshadowed a crucial role for Gollum, some part he might yet play in carrying out this mission. At Mount Doom, his part is revealed; he steals the ring from Frodo just as Frodo announces he doesn't have the strength to destroy it, but he falls into the flames in the process. Frodo's mission is complete, and the ring is destroyed.

Frodo collapses on the slopes of Mount Doom as it violently erupts, and eagles come to bear him and his companion, Sam, back to the house of the elves. Thought dead, and near it, he recovers and returns to the Shire.

Frodo isn't home when he returns to the Shire, though. His journey has utterly transformed him, and he is restless. His journey home is only complete when he sails west with the Elves to the Grey Havens, a place where the residual presence of the ring can be relieved.

Frodo is an unlikely hero in The Lord of the Rings. One might anticipate that the real hero would be Aragorn, the heir to the throne of Gondor who has lived in exile. Although Aragorn, too, undergoes a hero's journey, the true hero of the series is Frodo, who wins the war by his fortitude, his self-sacrifice, and his suffering.

His sacrifice comes from a deep well of inner strength. Gandalf has the rare ability to see strength hidden inside the small frames of the Hobbits. But it's not because Hobbits possess any magical ability; it's because of their very ordinariness. In *The Hobbit: An Unexpected Journey*, Gandalf says, "I have found it is the small everyday deeds of ordinary folk that keep the darkness at bay."[3]

It is the humanity (or maybe the hobbitity) of the Hobbits—their love of the land and friendship, their simplicity, their humble aspirations for a quiet life, a clean home, a good meal, and a comfortable bed—that is the source of their strength. Frodo, along with Sam, Merry, and Pippin, fight for the quiet dignity of life in the Shire, and it's Gandalf's view (and perhaps Tolkein's too) that these simple and ordinary aspirations are a wellspring for a deeper strength. The men who battle for the fate of Middle Earth fight for crowns and kingdoms, for fame and glory. But they show themselves too vain and too weak to bear the burden of the ring. The Hobbits suffer evil and violence on behalf of the rest of Middle Earth, but not for glory: they do it for the sake of the quiet lives they love and wish to preserve.

CHANNEL SURFING
The Dude as Suffering Servant

In the Old Testament Prophets, many passages predict the coming Messiah. Generally, these passages are divided into one of two categories: the Suffering Servant and the Son of David. These passages seem so different, so counterintuitive to one another, that many believed that the prophets spoke of two messiahs, not just one. One would come to suffer for Israel, bearing its sins, the other to redeem and rule it. Jesus did both, surprising everyone.

Looking at the Messiah through those two lenses deepens our understanding of Jesus's life and work. In movies and TV, we can see these two aspects of heroism, as well. Some (like most we're looking at in this chapter) are the Son of David type. They conquer enemies and establish new regimes.

But an example of the other—the Suffering Servant—is The Dude (Jeff Bridges), the hero of the Coen brothers' cult classic *The Big Lebowski*.

The Dude can be seen as a proto-messiah for a few reasons. There's the physical resemblance to popular images of Jesus. The Dude wears sandals and sports long hair, a beard, and a bathrobe in many scenes, and there's at least one overt reference in a dream sequence, where The Dude wears a carpenter's uniform. But more than that, there's his purpose on the earth. The Dude suffers on behalf of others.

The film begins with angry collectors breaking into The Dude's apartment and urinating on his rug when they discover that he doesn't have their money. The problem is, they're after the wrong guy. They want

Jeffrey Lebowski (Jeff Bridges), a man of means with a young, irresponsible wife. Instead, they've found Jeffrey Lebowski, a.k.a. The Dude, a man of leisure who doesn't do much at all.

In the unfolding story, The Dude is the subject of endless abuse but never strikes back. While he certainly isn't sinless (indeed, he has more than a few vices), his suffering is always on behalf of others. He is a proxy, or perhaps even a scapegoat, suffering for the other Lebowski, for Bunny Lebowski (Tara Reid), and for Walter's (John Goodman) anger and violence. His entire life is turned upside down because of the foolishness and deceptions of others. When the film ends, the narrator says, "The Dude Abides. I don't know about you but I take comfort in that. It's good knowing he's out there, The Dude . . . Taking it easy for all us sinners."[4]

Many won't identify with The Dude as Messiah, but some surely have. Innumerable websites are dedicated to the film and its many quotable moments, and Lebowski festivals have been held in cities all over the country. Something about The Dude strikes a chord, and like the narrator, people are comforted knowing he's out there, taking it easy for the rest of us.

THE JOURNEY OF SUPERMAN

Another hero who parallels the journey of Jesus came to the world in 1938, when Jerry Siegel and Joe Shuster revealed a character they had been developing for years: Superman. A hero who embodies all of humanity's highest ideals and aspirations, Superman is capable of almost every imaginable physical feat, vulnerable only to Kryptonite, and he has the impeccable character and virtue to match his power. The world of comics and pop culture at large has never been the same. As Grant Morrison, one of the great minds behind many contemporary comics and something of a philosopher of superheroes, wrote:

> Superman was the rebirth of our oldest idea. He was a god. His throne topped the peaks of an emergent dime store Olympus, and, like Zeus, he would disguise himself as a mortal to walk among the common people and stay in touch with their dramas and passions. . . . And as the opening caption of the Superman "origin" story from 1939 suggested—"AS A DISTANT PLANET WAS DESTROYED BY OLD AGE, A SCIENTIST PLACED HIS INFANT SON WITHIN A HASTILY DEVISED SPACE-SHIP, LAUNCH-ING IT TOWARD EARTH"—he was like the baby Moses or the Hindu Karna, set adrift in a basket on the river of destiny. And then there was the Western deity he best resembled: Superman was Christ, an unkillable champion sent down by his father (Jor-El) to redeem us by example and teach us how to solve our problems without killing one another.[5]

Superman has captivated imaginations ever since, in serials, movies, TV shows, and comic books. In spite of his absurd blue-and-red costume and his thinly veiled "secret identity" as Clark Kent, he remains utterly captivating, and in a strange way believable. We want someone like him to exist, someone who can end wars, who faces down bullets and bombs like they're harmless, and whose power is in good hands. We want someone we can trust to save the world.

While Superman's mythology has shifted over the years, certain themes remain constant.

His calling begins with his father, Jor-El, who sends his son to earth when their home planet is about to be destroyed. Jor-El knows that Kal-El (Superman) will not only carry on the legacy of his people, but will also be a beacon of hope for us mere humans.

But accepting the call is a challenge for young Kal-El. His spacecraft is found by Jonathan and Martha Kent, salt-of-the-earth farmers from Kansas, and they raise him with a heavy dose of middle-American humility. As he grows up, he's tried and tested, wrestling with his identity and his history. He is utterly alone, a stranger on earth and the last of his race. His powers make him even more foreign and alien, and he is tempted to deny and hide them. He runs for a while, but eventually has to face who he is. Craig Detweiler, writing about *Man of Steel* (Hollywood's most recent Superman film) described it like this: "As Clark Kent grows into manhood, he leans into his calling. His gifts are a burden, something he may have wanted to avoid. But no amount of hiding on a fishing boat can obscure the fact that Kal-El was created for more. His father, Jonathan Kent told him, 'You're not just anyone. One day, you're going to have to make a choice. You have to decide what kind of man you want to grow up to be. Whoever that man is, good character or bad, it's going to change the world.' Superman must make an active choice to stand up for goodness in the face of evil."[6]

He rises to the challenge. In fact, Superman has gone into the darkness and faced death again and again. In 1992, DC Comics ran three long series about the death (and resurrection) of Superman. A destroyer named Doomsday wreaked havoc, and only Superman had the strength and endurance to see the fight through to the end. The two battled to their mutual deaths. The world mourned Superman, and ultimately, four new heroes arose to take his place and wear the "S," continuing his legacy. He eventually returned (it required a complex plot involving a Kryptonian preserving and renewing his body), and discovered that upon conquering death, his powers were greater than ever before.

The Stories We Tell

In a different account, a graphic novel by Grant Morrison titled *All-Star Superman*, Lex Luthor manages to overexpose Superman to the sun's radiation. Superman's powers are greatly enhanced, but the radiation has overloaded his body's cells. He is going to die. The rest of the book is about Superman wrestling with mortality, saying good-bye to the people he loves, and wondering about his long-term legacy. It's a surprisingly thoughtful and poignant read.

What all Superman stories have in common—the movies in particular—is a moment of self-sacrifice. Superman's invulnerability and superstrength make him the target of wrath for every "bad guy" in the universe. They target him, the people he loves, and his city in hopes of dethroning him as the object of human hope and the ideal of perfection. In order to protect the world, he must constantly face death.

And we can always count on his willingness to go into the fray for us. Time and again, for almost a century, Superman descends into the darkness and faces the powers of evil on our behalf, rising again after risking life and limb, further cementing his emblem and image as objects of hope.

Coming home again, for Superman, means returning to his quiet life as Clark Kent. Clark isn't just a way for Superman to hide from the world; he is also a vision of Superman's true identity. He is both ideal man and everyman, which is to say that the ideal man *is* everyman. We can entrust Kal-El with his near-limitless power because he's also Clark Kent, the honest, humble farm boy from Kansas.

TOO MANY TO COUNT

We could follow similar trails all day.

One of my favorite heroes—one that seems to ring intentionally with Christian symbolism—is Prince Phillip, from Disney's *Sleeping Beauty*.

Called Away: He falls in love with a girl in the forest and announces to his father that he must marry the one he loves, not the one who is chosen for him (they happen to be the same girl).

Tried and Tested: He is captured and imprisoned by an evil sorceress, who has put his true love to sleep for one hundred years. The rest of the kingdom is also put to sleep, awaiting the resurrection of Sleeping Beauty.

Into the Darkness: He is armed with the Sword of Truth and the Shield of Virtue (the latter of which is marked with a cross) and fights his way through a forest of thorns (see Gen. 3:18) and a dragon (see Rev. 12:9).

Out of the Darkness: After conquering the dragon, he resurrects his bride with true love's kiss.

Home Again: Resurrecting Sleeping Beauty restores the kingdom to life and joy.

It's the gospel! The hero conquers the curse of sin and the monster of death in order to resurrect his bride and restore his kingdom.

In a more lighthearted vein, consider *Joe Versus the Volcano,* a 1990 romantic comedy starring Tom Hanks and Meg Ryan.

Called Away: After receiving a fatal prognosis for a brain disease, Joe (Tom Hanks) is invited by a billionaire to throw himself into a volcano as part of a business arrangement between the billionaire and the inhabitants of a Pacific island rich in minerals. Joe, when we meet him, is depressed and paranoid. To face the volcano, he will need to overcome his fear of death.

Tried and Tested: On the journey to the volcano, Joe faces a variety of obstacles. His ship sinks, and he falls in love with Patricia (Meg Ryan), the billionaire's daughter.

Into the Darkness: Joe must decide whether he's going to face the volcano. He decides he will, announcing his love for Patricia at the same time. They jump into the volcano together.

Out of the Darkness: The volcano erupts at the precise moment Patricia and Joe jump. They're knocked out of the volcano and into the ocean, where Joe's makeshift raft that spared their lives after the shipwreck awaits them. Joe, overwhelmed at being alive, remembers his brain disease. Recounting the details to Patricia, she realizes that Joe has been duped by her father; he isn't sick at all. Joe realizes that his whole life is ahead of him.

Home Again: Joe and Patricia set sail for home, Joe's fear of death conquered.

In yet another genre, there's Jason Bourne (Matt Damon). Let's just consider *The Bourne Identity*.

Called Away: Bourne's calling comes with amnesia. He doesn't know who he is or how he got there. This lapse in memory is what calls him away from "home" (his life as an assassin).

Tried and Tested: He goes on the run from his CIA supervisors, who send a number of his counterparts after him. Along the way he meets Marie (Franka Potente), and they begin a romance.

Into the Darkness: Bourne knows that in order to end the CIA's hunt for him, he must go to the very top of the organization he used to work for, called Treadstone. He has a confrontation with Conklin (Chris Cooper), the Treadstone director, and announces that he's leaving.

Out of the Darkness: Believing himself free, he leaves Conklin, escapes other assassins and disappears.

Home Again: He finds Marie renting scooters on an island in Greece, and they seem happy ever after. Bourne is ready to live a normal life, rather than the life of a killing machine.

One could go on and on. As a teaser to that effect, I've included the following chart.

	Jesus	Katniss (*The Hunger Games*)	Luke Sky-walker (Star Wars series)	Harry Potter
Called Away	The incarnation	Volunteers as Tribute in place of Prim	Invited by Obi-Wan to learn the ways of the force	Marked as a baby; "The boy who lived"
Tried and Tested	Temptations/ Gethsemane	Fights for her life in the Hunger Games	Battle of Yavin (first Death Star); Dagobah	Books 1–6
Into the Darkness	The cross	Prepares to commit suicide to deny the Game Masters their champion	Battle with Vader in Cloud City	Meeting Voldemort in the forbidden forest; Death
Out of the Darkness	The resurrection	Game Masters change the rules; Katniss and Peeta live	Battle with the Emperor at Endor	King's Cross Station; Resurrection
Home Again	The ascension	Returns to society as a symbol of rebellion and hope	Returns to the Alliance as a Jedi Master	Return to Hogwarts; Defeat of Voldemort

SEARCHING FOR HEROES IN THE BIBLE

When I was a teenager, I set out to read through the Bible. I was particularly interested in understanding manhood, and I began reading Genesis with an eye out for heroes. For many years, I'd heard in songs, sermons, and psalms about our heritage of faith, passed down from "Abraham, Isaac, and Jacob." In my mind, the men were carved in stone: brawny, fierce, and godly. Part of what excited me about reading their stories was the chance to learn something about manhood and marriage.

Boy was I surprised. These men were liars, weasels, cheaters, womanizers, and pimps.

The same character is revealed in the rest of the would-be heroes of the Old Testament. The closest thing we get is King

David, who slays giants and conquers armies, but who also commits adultery and coordinates a murder.

Even the disciples, I discovered, were bumbling and bickering, misunderstanding Jesus and his mission. Moments of heroic faith and revelation were counterpointed by moments of completely missing the point.

The absence of heroes in the Bible puzzled me for a long time. One day it dawned on me that perhaps this absence was the point of the whole book. There are no human heroes. Everyone's hands are stained and dirty. Had any of these men risen to the challenge and lived up to both God's standards and the standards of my imagination—the stone-carved heroism I'd expected to find—we wouldn't need the gospel. We wouldn't need Jesus. If we're honest with ourselves, we'll admit that in the shoes of David, Abraham, or Peter, we would probably be guilty of the same sins.

But the Bible isn't without a hero. Abraham doubts God's promises again and again—fathering a child through another woman and passing his wife off as his sister—and yet God keeps his promises. The story of the exodus isn't the story of Moses's heroism; it's the story of God's. David rose to greatness from his quiet, humble beginnings, but power birthed pride, which in turn birthed heinous sin. And still, God kept his promises, and through David, he sent the world the hero it longed for. He sent us Jesus, a human hero who identifies with every human element of frailty and weakness, but who transcends them, embodying our greatest desires and virtues as well.

For centuries, people have gathered and told tales meant to inspire hope and shed light on the struggles of life. They've told about men who conquered dragons and raised mountains, who rescued damsels and rose from the dead. Our hearts swell when we hear and see these stories—when we see Frodo escape from Mount Doom, or Iron Man cut off a portal to inter-galactic invaders. We cheer when Prince Phillip kisses Aurora and the kingdom comes to life again. We weep when Harry Potter rises from the dead, lifted by a deeper and older magic than even the most powerful wizard in the world can conjure: love. Then the theater lights lift and we return to the harsh daylight of the real world.

We can hear these stories of life, death, and resurrection, knowing in our hearts that it really did happen.

10

HONEY BOO BOO AND THE WEIGHT OF GLORY

We've become bored with watching actors that give us phony emotions.

Christof, *The Truman Show*

In 1973, PBS aired a groundbreaking show called *An American Family*. For seven months, producers and camera crews occupied the home of the Loud family, observing their ordinary and less-than-ordinary moments. In that period, Bill and Pat Loud separated and divorced, and their oldest son, Lance, came out as a homosexual.

The show was groundbreaking on many fronts. Lance was the first openly gay "character" on television, and the show paved the way for many imitators and follow-ups. It is the grandfather of reality television, and it was the seedling of the sentiment that reality TV has nurtured ever since. As Lance aptly described it, the show promoted the sentiment of "the middle-class dream that you can become famous for being just who you are."

Today, this same idea is often referred to as being "famous for nothing" or "famous for being famous." *An American*

Family opened the door to a new kind of celebrity, someone whose life was watched because of its ordinariness, and it opened the possibility of fame and glory for people whose lives and talents weren't necessarily noteworthy.

After *An American Family*, the concept simmered for a couple of decades, giving rise in the '90s to MTV's *The Real World*, a show about a handful of Generation Xers living in an apartment together. That show became an MTV staple, later inspiring *Road Rules*, a show about a handful of Generation Xers riding around in a Winnebago. These shows had moderate success, but were still a bit on the fringe of the mainstream.

When *Survivor* premiered in 2000, it lit a fire for reality programming, multiplying in a thousand ways. *Survivor* featured sixteen castaways divided into two tribes in a remote location in Borneo, where they were dropped and required to fend for themselves. They faced the challenges of the elements as well as the social challenges of living with one another. They faced group challenges for the first several weeks, tribe versus tribe, and in the later weeks, the tribes merged. Each week, one member of the tribe was voted off by the others. The physical challenges in these later weeks granted the victor individual immunity. One castaway, Kelly, won immunity several times in a row, but despite her physical dominance, she lost the vote in the final tribal council. Richard Hatch, a somewhat unlikeable character who spent a significant amount of time naked, won because of his psychological and strategic approach to the game. This set a standard that *Survivor* has largely maintained: the strategic game of relationships, alliances, and trust is far more important than the physical game.

Survivor was relatively cheap to produce and enormously popular, spawning a revolution in TV programming. Thirteen years later, reality TV is ubiquitous. Entire networks have based their programming on reality shows, featuring characters that do almost anything: run pawn shops, buy abandoned storage facilities, bake cupcakes, bake wedding cakes, size bras, sell houses, flip houses, redecorate houses, sell wedding dresses, and arrange marriages. We also have our choice of game-show-style reality contests: *The Amazing Race, Road Rules, Big Brother, Master Chef, The Next Food Network Star, Project Runway,* and more.

And, in true harmony with *An American Family,* plenty of shows feature people famous for doing nothing.

And so we turn to the topic of celebrity—the modern quest for glory—as we end the journey of the creation-fall-redemption-consummation arc. It's a pervasive cultural goal, almost perfectly illustrated by the modern phenomena of reality TV and social media.

The rise of social media has paralleled the explosive expansion of reality TV. Early platforms like Livejournal and Blogger gave way to MySpace, which in turn gave way to the dominant platforms we use today: Twitter, Google+, and of course, Facebook. And these are only a few examples. The web is crowded with platforms that intend to broaden our online connections and allow us (as YouTube might say) to broadcast ourselves to the world.

I don't think it's a coincidence that reality TV and social media have become dominant forces in American culture at the same time, though not necessarily because one caused the other. Instead, they're both products of an increasingly tech-saturated and narcissistic culture.

REALITY AND NARCISSISM

Reality TV has a bad reputation. It seems—in many ways—to be a breeding ground for a particularly potent kind of vanity and narcissism. In an informal study conducted by Dr. Drew Pinsky (of *Loveline* fame), celebrities scored higher than the

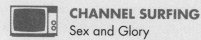 **CHANNEL SURFING**
Sex and Glory

In Genesis 2, sex was introduced into the world. What was meant to be a good (but mere) gift—a physical consummation of a whole-life union—has been twisted by sin. For many in our day, sex is the ultimate glory. We live in a culture that worships sexuality; we see this in the way sexual fulfillment is promised.

We simultaneously make too much of sex, holding it forth on one hand as the end-all, be-all of human existence (as Ferris Bueller might say), and cheapen it, treating it on the other hand as a commodity to be exchanged after a wayward glance, a brief greeting, or a wordless exchange of clicks and credit card numbers.

Sex, biblically, is like a covenantal renewal liturgy of marriage, an act that signifies all the other aspects of relationship that are part and parcel of marriage—honor and respect, love and service, conversations and chores. It flows out of the context of life: dinners, disasters, work, church, hospitals, schools, and parenting. It is meant to declare "you and no other," reorienting couples with an intimate and joyful act that sets their relationship apart from the rest of the world.

But a world that worships sex treats it like the idol of Isaiah 40, setting it up on the pedestals of our culture and saying, "Save me, you're my God!" In that world, sexuality becomes sovereign, a ruling appetite that dictates the way life should be lived. Lives become oriented around greater, better, more fulfilling experiences, trying to find satisfaction in something that will not be fully or finally satisfied, no matter how much or how often we feed it.

Pornography is a way of democratizing the quest for sexual fulfillment, making a pantheon of sexuality available for everyone. It is also a kind of sad, pathetic effort at redemption. It is a religious event, where sacrifices are made of money and dignity, and the god of fornication promises to the priests (the porn stars and filmmakers) fame and wealth, and to the acolytes (the consumers) a transcendent and satisfying sexual experience, something "hot," "raw," and "real" that is otherwise unavailable in their ordinary and often lonesome lives. But again, it's only as satisfying as a meal, and the appetite will need to be fed again and again.

We should note that Christians, too, place sex on a pedestal. How many Christian books treat sex as though it's the ultimate key to a happy marriage and a happy life? (I can think of two that were published just in the last year.) We should ask ourselves carefully, are the stories we tell as Christians about sex taking their cues from a sex-obsessed culture, or from the Scriptures? Is the way we talk about sex identical to the way the world talks about it? Are we thinking about marital union and covenant in a way that prepares marriages for hard times, for the natural decay of bodies with age, and for the very real possibilities of illness or injury that can leave one or the other partner without the ability to perform? If sex is the unifying center of marriage, then what happens when sex isn't possible—for a season or a lifetime?

As an ultimate hope, sexual gratification is destined to disappoint and frustrate, and believers need to pay attention to the kinds of stories they're telling—even among themselves—about sex, satisfaction, and ultimate joy.

general population on a test designed to diagnose Narcissistic Personality Disorder (or NPD). Not only that, he found that the highest scores of the two hundred people who took the test came from reality stars, not Hollywood actors.

As psychologists Jean Twenge and Keith Campbell comment on the phenomenon: "Reality TV shows, often the majority of the highest-rated shows, are a showcase of narcissism, making materialistic, vain, and antisocial behavior seem normal."[1]

There is, of course, a spectrum to that kind of behavior on television, with normal-seeming folks like the Roloffs (stars of *Little People, Big World*) at one end of the spectrum and the spectacularly abnormal at the other (any version of *Real Housewives*). Perhaps the most mainstream and pervasive celebrity family is broadcast on *Keeping Up with the Kardashians*.

Kim Kardashian was born into Hollywood aristocracy. Her father is a famous trial lawyer and friend to the stars. Her stepfather is Olympian Bruce Jenner. She was working as a stylist to another reality television star, Paris Hilton. Then, in 2007, her sex tape was released.

Several years earlier, she had filmed explicit videos while dating a singer named Ray-J. He sold the footage to a pornography distributor, and its release became big news. The scandal around the tape, Kim's lawsuit against the distributor, and its viral popularity on the web made her name front-page news. Shortly after, filming began on the reality series featuring Kim and her family, *Keeping Up with the Kardashians*.

Over the years, viewers have watched Kim build an empire around herself and her family. They have clothing lines, fashion boutiques, a host of endorsements, and spinoff shows. Her mother now hosts a talk show. Kim famously got engaged to basketball player Kris Humphries, had a massive televised wedding, and filed for divorce seventy-two days later. More recently, she's been dating Kanye West and given birth to her first child, North "Nori" West. She's appeared in a handful of movies and TV shows, none of which revealed any hidden talent, and she's appeared on innumerable magazine covers.

The Kardashians make no apologies for their fame. In this excerpt from an interview in *The Guardian*, Kim seems puzzled at the criticism she's received:

> "When I hear people say [what are you famous for?], I want to say, what are you talking about?" she says slowly, her eyes wide as a bushbaby's. "I have a hit TV show. We've shot more episodes than I Love Lucy! We've been on the air longer than The Andy Griffith Show! I mean, these are iconic shows, so it blows my mind when people say that."
>
> But you're not performing; you're just being followed around by cameras . . .
>
> "But to be able to open up your life like that and to be so . . . if everyone could do it, everyone would. It doesn't make sense to me." . . .
>
> For the record then, what is Kardashian's talent?
>
> "What is my talent?" She cocks her head to one side. "Well, a bear can juggle and stand on a ball and he's talented, but he's not famous. Do you know what I mean?"[2]

Fame and fabulousness should be enough, right? In the world of reality TV, it is. The real skill the Kardashians demonstrate is the ability to manage publicity. They are famous because they're perpetually in the news for being famous. They are on the A-list because they're A-listers. To shift perspective a little, we watch them because everyone is watching them. Their skill is that they're eminently watchable.

Certainly the fact that the Kardashian family is wealthy, glamorous, and beautiful plays into their staying power, but they're far from the only family with those credentials. It's their willingness to put their lives on display and their skill in packaging that display—taping the right moments, managing "real life" conversations before the cameras—that give them staying power in the news and tabloids.

Kim's brand of fame has generated no small amount of criticism. Will Smith, when asked about how his family's fame compared to the Kardashians', said: "Fame is almost an inconsequential by-product of what we're really trying to accomplish. We are trying to put great things into the world, we're trying to have fun, and we're trying to become the greatest versions of ourselves in the process of doing things we love. So the idea of fame or exploitation or orchestrating the media is sometimes even less than desirable for us."[3] For Smith, the work comes first. Fame should follow great work; it's not an end in itself.

Smith is far from alone in this sentiment. Actor Daniel Craig said, "Look at the Kardashians, they're worth millions. Millions! I don't think they were that badly off to begin with, but now look at them. You see that and you think, 'What, you mean all I have to do is behave like a @#$% *idiot* on television and then you'll pay me millions?' I'm not judging it. . . . well, I am *obviously*."[4]

Jon Hamm, star of *Mad Men*, had several public exchanges with Kim Kardashian after saying, "Whether it's Paris Hilton or Kim Kardashian or whoever, stupidity is certainly celebrated. . . . Being a @#$% idiot is a valuable commodity in this culture because you're rewarded significantly."[5]

Kardashian replied, "We're all working hard and we all have to respect one another. Calling someone who runs their own businesses, is a part of a successful TV show, produces, writes, designs, and creates, 'stupid,' is in my opinion careless."[6]

Hamm replied again, "It's surprising to me that it has become remotely a story. . . . I don't know Ms. Kardashian, I know her public persona. What I said was meant to be more on pervasiveness of something in our culture, not personal, but she took offense to it and that is her right."[7]

In a later interview, he said, "My quote was simply about that version of television and that version of American culture being celebrated and it's not something that I particularly enjoy."[8]

It's an interesting contrast. *Mad Men*, Hamm's show, treats glamour, fame, and beauty as a veneer, something to mask the darkness and sadness of our true selves. *Keeping Up with the Kardashians* treats the same material as the goal of life and work. Kardashian can't understand the criticism: "We're . . . working hard," she says, referring to the tremendous amount of energy that goes into sustaining the empire associated with her name. For her, the proof is in the resulting dollar signs, the presence in the news, the number of Twitter followers. But Hamm's problem (and Craig's and Smith's) is not in the dollars and cents; it's the product itself. It's the promotion of the veneer.

ANOTHER FACE OF "REALITY"

Of course, not all reality television is about being fabulous. Not all reality stars live in million-dollar homes, get laser treatments for hair removal, and drive around in Land Rovers. There is an entirely different kind of "reality," and the poster child for this vein of entertainment is a girl named Honey Boo Boo.

Here Comes Honey Boo Boo launched after the show's namesake and her mother appeared on another reality show, *Toddlers and Tiaras*. This show features the incredibly competitive and incredibly strange world of child beauty pageants. In a world that was already weird, Honey Boo Boo and Mama June stood out as yet a degree weirder. The brash, Mountain Dew–swilling, crude persona of Honey Boo Boo, along with her equally brash and crude mother, seemed like a gold mine for its cable network, and shortly after their episode of *Toddlers* ran, they began filming their own show.

Filmed in rural McIntyre, Georgia, *Here Comes Honey Boo Boo* features Alana "Honey Boo Boo" Thompson; her mother, "Mama June" Shannon; her father, Mike "Sugar Bear" Thompson; and her sisters, Lauren, Anna, and Jessica. The show centers primarily on Mama June, following her as she preps Honey Boo Boo for pageants and buys junk food at auctions. The family lives in poverty and embodies (quite literally) many of the problems that perpetuate poverty: poor nutrition, obesity, undereducation, underemployment, and teen pregnancy.

It would have been possible to do documentary work on this family that humanized them and evoked sympathy, but that clearly is not the intent of the show's producers. An early episode brought an etiquette teacher to work with Honey Boo Boo and her sister, trying to teach them such basics as "don't fart at the dinner table." The girls' response, of course, made it clear that they had no interest in learning new habits.

As Ryan McGee, a critic for the online magazine *The AV Club*, wrote of the episode: "It's not the pair failing to transform into princesses after one session that is depressing. It's that the show presents even the very idea of them being able to reach a point at which not farting at the table is even possible as a totally improbable idea."[9]

The show thrives on featuring the saddest elements of this family's life. Their bad parenting, bad manners, bad eating habits, hypocritical mockery of others who are poor or overweight, and indifferent attitude toward one daughter's teenage pregnancy—all happening alongside the Technicolor wackiness of child beauty pageants (complete with 300-plus-pound Mama June dancing in sync with Honey Boo Boo from the audience)—is treated as comic, not tragic. It's televisual cannibalism, feasting on the bones of this family in a combination of laughs and wide-eyed disbelief—the kind that usually occurs when driving past a traffic accident.

The widespread success of the show speaks to broader cultural attitudes about the South and about political correctness. Apparently, it's okay to hold up this family and their problems—many of which are broad, systemic social problems like education, poverty, and obesity—for laughs and ridicule.

VIEWING AND JUDGMENT

It strikes me that this vulture-like attitude is at the heart of most reality consumption. *Honey Boo Boo* requires an audience that is detached and disinterested, able to judge and laugh. If you think too hard about what you're seeing—the express train to diabetes, teen pregnancy, and perpetuated poverty and ignorance—it becomes painful and sad. But the production is designed to never let you think too hard, accompanying the action with a cartoon-like soundtrack that accents every stumble, jiggle, and stutter.

A disinterested attitude is also required for watching more mundane-seeming shows like *The Amazing Race*, *Survivor*, and *Project Runway*. Where would those shows be without ridiculous, obnoxious personalities, like the husband who screams at his wife on *The Amazing Race* or the emotional basket case on *Runway*.

Consider the Gordon Ramsay television empire: *MasterChef*, *Hell's Kitchen,* and *Kitchen Nightmares*. Ramsay has made an art of berating and humiliating the people on his shows. Viewers vicariously participate in that judgment or cheer for the show's contestants, thereby judging Ramsay for his treatment of them.

Even *Keeping Up with the Kardashians* invites judgment. The show highlights aspects of the family's life that demonstrate how spoiled, pampered, and detached they are from real life. It's not hard to feel indignant, particularly when Kim is known for saying things like, "I hate when women wear the wrong foundation color, it might be the worst thing on the planet when they wear their make up too light."[10]

Reality programming strikes us differently than fictional programming. The over-the-top behavior of characters on sitcoms or soap operas is always buffered in our minds because we know it isn't real. Watching "reality" unfold is entirely different, inviting a deeper scrutiny and inevitable comparisons. "I can't believe people live like that." "I can't believe he treats her that way."

Reality TV reminds us of the daytime talk shows from the late '80s and early '90s, shows like *The Jerry Springer Show*, *The Sally Jessy Raphael Show*, and *The Donahue Show*, whose hosts competed to find the most bizarre guests. These shows are best described by "Weird Al" Yankovic's lampoon of them in the film *UHF*, wherein he hosted a talk show called *Town Talk* featuring "Lesbian Nazi Hookers, abducted by UFOs and Forced into Weight-Loss Programs." This would have been a believable subject on *Sally* or *Donahue*.

If you think about it, any effort to tell "real" and "true" stories on television is going to gravitate toward the extremes; real life is simply too boring. In fact, real life is so boring, we'd *rather* be watching TV. The same is true in movies. Don Miller's book *A Million Miles in a Thousand Years* recounts the journey of making his memoir, *Blue Like Jazz*, into a film. Early on in the process, the filmmakers bring up the awkward reality that the movie will have to be spiced up; Don's life is simply too boring for movie audiences.

> "Let me put it this way," Steve [the producer] said. "While you've written a good book, *thoughts* don't translate onto the screen very well. They will be restless. They won't engage . . ."

"You think they might be bored if we just show my life the way it is," I clarified. I guess I was asking for reassurance that my life was okay.

"I think they'd stab each other in the necks with drinking straws," Steve said.[11]

TV and movies must gravitate toward the superlative, the extremes, or else they won't hold our attention. In fictional shows, that's done easily. The hero always wins, the bad guy always loses, and the good guy always gets the girl—and all of that happens in appropriate intervals of time. In reality programming, the stories are harder to manipulate (though certainly a lot of manipulation goes on) and producers and programmers have to depend on the characters themselves being larger than life. Thus, people from the fringes of our culture— the oddities and outliers—end up taking center stage.

These characters are then framed, packaged, and beamed into our living rooms where we can oversee their judgment with impunity.

REALITY TV AND SOCIAL MEDIA

Often, when we see shows like *Honey Boo Boo*, we wonder what would motivate the stars to put their lives on display and up for scrutiny. The money is an obvious motivator, but is money enough to explain the impulse?

I don't think it is. I think something deeper is going on for both Honey Boo Boo and the Kardashians, and if we're honest, it motivates all of us. It's the same motivator that has caused social media to explode in the last ten years.

One way to understand social media is as a vehicle for self-broadcasting. When we post on Facebook, Twitter, and Instagram, we're projecting an image of ourselves to the world. Just as *Keeping Up with the Kardashians* is carefully planned and edited to shape the family's image and brand, so is our social

CHANNEL SURFING
Where Everybody Knows Your Name

One thing I've discovered as a pastor is that most people feel lonely. Friendships are never easy. Whenever we live in proximity to others—whether friends or family—we come in contact with one another's sins. Generally, our experiences of friendship have an ebb and flow. They change seasonally as we grow weary with one another and seek a little space and distance.

The TV sitcom is a comfort for our insecurities about friendships. On *Cheers*, you're invited to join the community at a place "where everybody knows your name." *Friends* is set in New York City, one of the most transient places on earth, featuring characters who—in spite of busy careers—always have time for one another. It's downright utopian.

Even *Seinfeld*, whose characters were largely despicable, had a kind of enduring commitment to one another.* *Arrested Development* has the same enduring kind of bond; no matter how dark and how terrible the relationships get, the characters always seem to arrive at a place of peace and connection.

In all of these stories, no sin is too great, no hurt so painful that it can break up the characters' unspoken commitment to one another. It is, in an odd way, a reflection of the church, where people come together from different backgrounds, where we forebear one another's sins, and where we share burdens of suffering.

---

*See page 102, Channel Surfing: Why Seinfeld's Final Episode Was Perfect.

media presence. Your Facebook timeline is your version of a reality show.

In 2011, when Facebook launched its "timeline" feature, founder Mark Zuckerberg described his company's mission as making "the world more open and connected."[12] Timeline's goal was to provide "a new way to express who you are."[13] Technology becomes a vehicle for more than just communication; it's about expression of identity. It's a way we invite others into our lives and our stories. Beyond that, technology invites a way of relating in the world. Tweeting, updating, texting, scrolling through updates, taking selfies—these become the dominant relational habits of our lives.

Our presence on social media is a story we're telling about who we are, and like the production of a reality TV show, it's all about the editing. What we share and don't share on social media is shaped by how we want the world to see us. With the click of a button, we can open and close doors of connectivity. No awkward conversations. Rare repercussions. Easily managed, easily edited lives.

Social media also provides a profound illusion; our mobile devices are designed to make us feel like the whole digital world is all about us. Our tailored choices about who we want to hear from (and who we don't) are in place already. We open an app and feel "connected," when in fact we haven't connected at all; we've actually disconnected from the people immediately around us.

Sherry Turkle, a sociologist who studies technology's impact on society, notes the way we have shifted from conversation to "connection"—from face-to-face interaction to device-mediated interaction. In a *New York Times* op-ed, she writes:

> Texting and e-mail and posting let us present the self
> we want to be. This means we can edit. And if we wish to,

we can delete. Or retouch: the voice, the flesh, the face, the body. Not too much, not too little—just right.

Human relationships are rich; they're messy and demanding. We have learned the habit of cleaning them up with technology. And the move from conversation to connection is part of this. But it's a process in which we shortchange ourselves. Worse, it seems that over time we stop caring, we forget that there is a difference.[14]

Remarkably, the creators of Facebook seem to revel in the power of this shift. A series of commercials promoting a Facebook-branded mobile device showed individuals "escaping" social situations by stealing glimpses at their smartphone. A girl at a family meal tuned out her grandmother's talking and scrolled through pictures. The room was transformed as she surfed, letting her avoid her family and feel present at a friend's snowball fight. It gives the impression that the phone makes one as good as there. In another ad, a girl walking through an art museum with classical paintings and sculptures escapes through her phone as well, transforming the art into (among other things) pictures of her friends taking selfies.

At any moment, we can escape into a private world that's tailored to us and that is eager for our next picture, our next status update, our next link—a world complete with a built-in system of rewards for worthy content: retweets, likes, and so on. On the web, we all star in our own show. We glory in ourselves.

DESIRE, SOCIAL MEDIA, AND REALITY TV

As far as I'm concerned, the world doesn't need another condemning rant about social media or reality television. I'm not saying the criticism is undeserving—my own read on them probably doesn't veil my distaste for them very well. But that's not my goal here.

Instead, in a way that I hope is consistent with the rest of this book, I want to look behind these stories and ask how they might connect to the bigger story. Is the desire to broadcast ourselves in either venue somehow connected to the bigger story of creation, fall, redemption, and consummation?

Our first impulse might be to say, "Of course not." Isn't this all a manifestation of pride? Isn't a narcissistic culture the antithesis of the gospel?

To that I'd say yes . . . and no.

This desire to put ourselves on display is antithetical to the degree that we see it as a means to ultimate happiness. If we think fame, fortune, followers, likes, comments, retweets, and favorites are going to satisfy our souls, we're absolutely wrong.

But is there a kind of praise, a kind of fame, and a kind of self-glorification that we might seek for good purposes?

To properly understand the whole story of the gospel, we must remember the bookends of creation and consummation. We live with a hopeful eye toward a day when things will return to the way they were meant to be. And part of that destiny is restored glory. We were once the crown of creation, bearing God's image, carriers of a tremendous glory and beauty. One day, those who are in Christ will have that glory restored, but until then, we feel what we've lost and what we long for. Christian and non-Christian alike feel the dull ache of faded glory.

So we fill our days with efforts at transcending that ache.

C. S. Lewis described this ache better than anyone else. He understood our desires as being rooted in creation, but misdirected. In an oft-quoted passage from his essay, "The Weight of Glory," he writes:

> Indeed, if we consider the unblushing promises of reward
> and the staggering nature of the rewards promised in the
> Gospels, it would seem that Our Lord finds our desires not

too strong, but too weak. We are half-hearted creatures, fooling about with drink and sex and ambition when infinite joy is offered us, like an ignorant child who wants to go on making mud pies in a slum because he cannot imagine what is meant by the offer of a holiday at the sea. We are far too easily pleased.[15]

It's not that the hunger for glory or even fame is wrong; it's that we're too easily satisfied. Lewis himself wrestled with whether a "godly" desire for fame was possible, but in his study of the meaning of *glory*, he came to see that "fame or good report" was actually the best definition. Biblically, what we seek is fame that comes from appreciation by God. Lewis calls it "the divine accolade, 'Well done, thou good and faithful servant.'"[16]

There is something innately good, natural, and childlike in wanting to be praised for who we are and what we've done. We were made for glory; after God created us, he said we were "good." We long to hear him tell us this again; we long for an affirmation that who we are and what we are is "good." All of the rewards of social media, all of the fans and followers we might collect as reality TV celebrities, pale in comparison to the glory that awaits the children of God when we hear the divine affirmation of our redeemed goodness.

When the desire for glory becomes twisted, when we ultimately desire the praise of men, it turns ugly. Lewis wrote: "I am not forgetting how horribly this most innocent desire is parodied in our human ambitions, or how very quickly, in my own experience, the lawful pleasure of praise from those whom it was my duty to please turns into the deadly poison of self-admiration."[17] But such sin is always a corruption and a misdirection of a deeper, better, and older longing. It's the longing of creature for Creator, of bride for Groom, of child for Father. We long for an ultimately satisfying embrace that welcomes us as we are for who we are.

In his book *The Art of Fiction*, novelist John Gardner argues that the most important feature of any story is profluence. A story must have a locomotion of its own, a trajectory. It requires a sense of forward motion and destination. Gardener writes, "The writer distracts the readers—breaks the film if you will—when by some slip of technique or egoistic intrusion he allows or forces the reader to stop thinking about the story (stop 'seeing' the story) and think about something else."[18]

You might say this trajectory is about the attention of the audience; they won't stick with you if your story isn't going somewhere. There's certainly some truth in that assessment, but I believe that this need for forward motion in a story is rooted in reality. Most people think that life means something and that it is going somewhere, and they live life with a sense of destination.

Reality TV follows a trajectory to the glory of the red carpet and the Neilsen ratings. The forward motion of social media involves accumulating fans, friends, and followers. They both aim at a kind of glory that scratches a deeply human itch, but in a way that is ultimately unsatisfying.

The gospel tells us that life, indeed, is heading somewhere. There's an end to the story, and it's an end that by God's grace can be an experience of the greatest good and the most satisfying glorification that we'll ever know.

Only that embrace will truly satisfy us, in that moment when sin's stain is removed and, as Lewis puts it, "The door on which we have been knocking all our lives will open at last."[19]

May we never settle for anything less.

EPILOGUE

(And a Word to Christian Filmmakers)

It's been about a year since I began writing this book. I must admit, the journey has surprised me several times. I've been surprised by what I've learned, occasionally surprised by boredom, and often surprised by connections between stories and ideas that I hadn't seen before.

When I neared the finish line, I realized that in many ways this book is the perfect partner (or in movie-geek style, this book could be the *prequel*) to my previous book, *Rhythms of Grace: How the Church's Worship Tells the Story of the Gospel.* Now to be sure, this isn't a Gallagher moment; I am not here at the end of this book trying to sell you something. But I think it's worth saying a few things about *Rhythms* in light of *The Stories We Tell.*

I've intentionally tried to view the stories in this book in the light of the gospel, treating their characters, plots, and images as signposts for a truth that the writers, directors, and actors might not even be aware of, but that we all, nonetheless, long for. I've done that—and I believe you can too—because I believe the big story of creation, fall, redemption, and consummation is the *primary* story in the world. It's a story whose impact is so powerful, so pervasive, and so deeply connected to human nature that we can't help but riff on it when we tell stories of our own.

It's not the only way to read these stories. For instance, one could see from Quentin Tarantino's films that he glories too much in violence. You would be right. One could see that the hopelessness of *The Wire* is despairing and potentially destructive. You would be right about that, too. And many of these stories glory in bad language or drug use, or in a reckless lack of self-control.

The fact is that these stories are far from Christian, and they offer varying visions of ultimate hope. Love stories can be signposts for God's love for his people, but they also can be seen as stories that find ultimate hope in romantic love. Tarantino seems to find ultimate hope in vengeance. Reality TV finds ultimate hope in celebrity. Makeover shows find ultimate hope in beauty. Viewed in this way, these stories are like liturgies.

A *liturgy* is the work of the people. It's something we gather together to do. In the church, the liturgy is the work of remembering and embodying the gospel story together. It's the work of gathering, reading Scripture, singing, praying, preaching, feasting, and sending.

Our stories in movies and TV are liturgical in the sense that they tell stories of ultimate hope. They gather us with a song (opening credits) and send us out with a rejoinder to return next week ("Stay tuned for scenes from our next episode"). In between these bookends, they present problems and solutions. Occasionally, the kind of ultimate hope they advocate is voiced overtly, with stories of "this changed my life" (makeover shows, talk shows, etc.), but mostly their messages are much more subtle.

To bring us full circle here, I'll quote James K. A. Smith again, who's book *Desiring the Kingdom* examines the liturgical shape of all of life, including TV and movies. Smith notes one example, saying:

> One of the things that liturgies do is to visibly narrate a story about what really matters. . . . Perhaps one of the more prolific examples . . . is found in the work of Jerry Bruck-

heimer, the producer of a wide range of films (and more recently television dramas) that draw upon and present the ideals of Americanism. . . . Though I can't offer a complete analysis here, I raise the case of Bruckheimer in order to suggest that, once again, a space (namely the cinema) that we might have considered neutral or indifferent (or perhaps eagerly affirmed as "good" and "creational") is formative in a liturgical sense: here we have moving icons dancing across the screen bathed in the affect of a calculated sound track, staging a story with implicit visions of the good life that, over time and because of their covert nature, seep into our imagination and shape not only how we see the world but also how we relate to it, how we orient ourselves within it, and what we ultimately are working toward.[1]

What Smith argues is that these liturgies—like the church's—have a shaping impact on our lives. They are formative. They shape how we see and act in the world because they demonstrate a way of living in the world that promises (truly or falsely) satisfaction. "The good life," as Smith says.

By themselves, these stories will lead to despair. The things they promise can't fulfill us, and if we live only with them, we will find ourselves feeling drained and empty.

Which brings me to *Rhythms of Grace*. The story the world truly longs to hear is the story of the gospel. The ultimate hope that actually satisfies is restoration with God, and for almost two millennia, the people of God have gathered and remembered that story together. It's the truer, better story that we've longed to hear for our entire lives.

Remarkably, in the light of the gospel, these other stories become brighter and more encouraging. They are signposts, altars to an unknown god, and like Paul, we can say, "Yes, indeed! But it's even better than you thought." When you see the bigger story, these others aren't diminished, but are held in their proper place. In fact, they become more beautiful and more interesting.

When we understand that the context of human life on earth is this bigger story, we discover a three-dimensional view of every story, every work of art, and every person we meet. Whether we know it or not, we're all working at salvation. We are living and acting in ways that attempt to give life meaning and purpose. Storytellers are probing at how we got into this mess of a world, noticing the wonders it contains, and imagining possibilities that might make the world better, or might make us happier in the midst of it.

Sometimes they aim far too low. Sometimes they strike awfully near the truth. Sometimes, they simply despair. What they hold in common is a belief that the world is a really interesting place. It's worth talking about and wondering about. It's worth exploring and reimagining.

THE WONDER OF HUMANITY

The one thing that ties all stories together—from the most grim indie film to the silliest comedies, from Disney cartoons to *The Wire*—is their humanity. The story arcs of so many TV shows, books, movies, and comics are common to all people, and what separates the bad from the good from the great is their success in revealing believable and interesting characters. Great stories are deeply human stories, introducing us to people with whom we want to journey.

As C. S. Lewis put it, "There are no ordinary people. You have never talked to a mere mortal. Nations, cultures, arts, civilisations—these are mortal, and their life is to ours as the life of a gnat. But it is immortals whom we joke with, work with, marry, snub, and exploit—immortal horrors or everlasting splendours."[2]

We are made in God's image, reflectors and carriers of some part of God's own immeasurable goodness and grace. Even in our sin-scarred brokenness, we can't help but reflect—however dimly—some part of that goodness. Humanity is infinitely interesting because it is a reflection of an infinitely interesting God.

Jack Kerouac beautifully captured that ethos in *On the Road*. Kerouac was part of the Beat Generation, a postwar writer who felt disenfranchised, uninterested in chasing the American dream. While his life lacked typical ambitions, it never lacked joy and curiosity. When he meets the charismatic Dean Moriarty for the first time, Kerouac finds himself captivated, and in a famous quote, he describes Moriarty (and Carlo Marx), who:

> danced down the streets like dingledodies, and I shambled after as I've been doing all my life after people who interest me, because the only people for me are the mad ones, the ones who are mad to live, mad to talk, mad to be saved, desirous of everything at the same time, the ones that never yawn or say a commonplace thing, but burn, burn, burn like fabulous yellow roman candles exploding like spiders across the stars and in the middle you see the blue center-light pop and everybody goes "Awww!"[3]

Life is full of these people. We befriend them, marry them, and give birth to them. Sometimes, we are them.

Storytelling is a great gift because humanity is a great gift, something God himself delights in. When we engage great stories, we engage with people, seeing ourselves reflected in their desires and faults. If the big story of creation, fall, redemption, and consummation is the background of all of our stories, then humanity is the common foreground—broken image-bearers trying to make sense of life.

A WORD TO (ASPIRING) CHRISTIAN FILMMAKERS

We sometimes assume that a Christian artist's worldview should result in overtly "Christian" content. In filmmaking this means we expect Christians to create Christian cinema as a genre or a subculture of its own (like Christian Contemporary Music), focusing on strongly redemptive and openly evangelistic or biblical story lines (e.g., *Fireproof* and the Left Behind series).

In other vocations, we rarely make the same requirement. Most of us aren't concerned about whether a homebuilder sees all the world under the rule and reign of God, and we're much less concerned about being able to see the gospel in his work. We're far more concerned with whether the builder has character and can be trusted. We would not expect an engineer to work an ichthus into each of his designs, but (metaphorically speaking) we expect exactly that out of Christian artists, filmmakers, and musicians.

The alternative to this cloistered, subculture-nurturing attitude is to challenge all Christians to excel in their respective industries, whether they're teachers, plumbers, tap dancers, or filmmakers. As James Davison Hunter argues in *To Change the World*, if we want to exercise influence in culture, we need to go to the institutions where it's most profoundly shaped.[4] Instead of standing outside (in a subculture) and speaking in, we need truly excellent artists to go into the heart of cultural production—in this case, the Hollywood and New York film scenes—transforming it from the inside out.

Filmmakers are storytellers, and Christian filmmakers should (vocationally speaking) focus first and foremost on telling great stories. Works by C. S. Lewis and J. R. R. Tolkien have stood the test of time and gained influence not because of their theology but because of the quality of their storytelling. Their theology informed their worldview, and certainly it shaped their portrayal of humanity, but it wasn't the driving force of their stories. In fact, in Tolkien's introduction to a later edition of The Lord of the Rings trilogy, he says he despises allegory and fiercely argues that his goal in the development of the series was to create a believable world and tell a compelling story. That should be an end itself.

The heart of great stories is always great characters, and that's as true with Lewis and Tolkein as it is with Cormac Mc-Carthy or Martin Scorsese. It's why shows like *Seinfeld* endure today. It's also the secret to reality television; the premise of the show rarely matters. People watch because they like watching people.

The thing that separates McCarthy from the *Real Housewives* or *Mad Men* from *Two and a Half Men* is the degree to which they explore the complexity of being human. Our better stories remind us that we are both sinners *and* image-bearers, capable of good and even brilliant things, but also flawed to the core.

Christian storytellers shouldn't be afraid of that complexity. In fact, they should be the first ones to dive neck-deep into it.

Preachiness in films is always obnoxious, whether it's from evangelicals or Michael Moore. People go to the theater hoping to watch a compelling story. When an artist's urge to get a message across trumps the need to tell a good story, the film suffers and the audience cries foul. They came for an adventure and they got a sermon. But this is exactly what many Christians think of when they talk about "Christian" filmmaking.

A good story, as I've argued in this book, can carry profound redemptive themes and portray the agonies and ecstasies of everyday life in ways that a sermon can't (not to say that stories are superior; they're just different). Telling good stories doesn't require conscious attention to redemptive themes nearly as much as it requires believable, quality writing, acting, and production. Capture a few really human moments. Show us someone who gloriously reflects God's brilliance, but is utterly broken by sin. Tell me a story that I can identify with, one that features someone as broken as I am, who longs for redemption and seeks it out, for better or worse, in the earthy circumstances of ordinary life.

If Christians who knew how to tell great stories could gain positions of influence in the centers of filmmaking, they could positively influence the culture of film. They could tell better stories and show the viability and plausibility of faith in a world that denies it.

They would gain a foothold in the contemporary imagination that has subtle but strong influence on the formation of attitudes and habits in our culture. They could change the norms for what's acceptable or required in serious films. It's sad that great shows on cable television and films that want to compete in the Oscar race are compelled to achieve a certain level of sexuality in order to be taken seriously. (This is a broad generalization, of course, but it serves to illustrate a place where change could occur.)

So how do we get there? This is the fun part.

They say that anything worth doing is worth doing badly. This is as true of filmmaking as it is of anything, and it's the final thing I'll say to a Christian who wants to be the next Spielberg or Soderbergh. If you want to make films, then make films. Make them badly. Make them with iPhones and flip cameras, edit them on a laptop or in a computer lab at your middle school. Make lots of them, and don't worry about whether they're any good until you've made ten or twenty. Even then, don't worry when they're bad. Look for the things you've done well and figure out how to apply those lessons to the entire next project. Keep going and pressing on in your spare time. Chase down the craft of storytelling like you're stalking prey in the woods. You'll start with just glimpses in the underbrush—evidence that you're close, a flash of it here and there. Keep at it, and someday you'll catch one.

WORKS CITED

Abrams, J. J., Jeffrey Lieber, and Damon Lindelof, writers. "Through the Looking Glass." *Lost*. ABC. May 23, 2007.

Augustine. *The Confessions of St. Augustine*. Translated by E. B. Pusey. New York: P. F. Collier Son, 1909.

Berry, Wendell. *That Distant Land: The Collected Stories*. Washington, DC: Shoemaker Hoard, 2004.

The Big Lebowski. Directed by Ethan Coen and Joel Coen. Performed by Jeff Bridges and John Goodman. PolyGram Filmed Entertainment, 1998.

Brockes, Emma. "Kim Kardashian: My Life as a Brand." Theguardian.com. September 7, 2012. http://www.theguardian.com/lifeandstyle/2012/sep/07/kim-kardashian-life-as-brand.

Carter, Chris, writer. "Clyde Bruckman's Final Repose." *The X-Files*. Fox. October 13, 1995.

————. "Jose Chung's 'From Outer Space.'" *The X-Files*. Fox. April 12, 1996.

Coming to America. Directed by John Landis. Performed by Eddy Murphy and Arsenio Hall. Paramount Pictures, 1988. DVD.

Cosper, Mike. "The 3 Most Disturbing Words on TV." *The Gospel Coalition* (blog). November 22, 2010. http://thegospelcoalition.org/blogs/tgc/2010/11/22/the-3-most-disturbing-words-on-tv/.

Crash. Directed by Paul Haggis. Performed by Don Cheadle and Ludacris. Lions Gate Films, 2005.

David, Larry, and Jerry Seinfeld, writers. "The Finale." *Seinfeld*. NBC. May 14, 1998.

The Descendants. Directed by Alexander Payne. Performed by George Clooney and Shailene Woodley. Twentieth Century Fox, 2011.

Detweiler, Craig. *Man of Steel: Jesus—The Original Superhero*. Sermon Notes. MinistryResources.org, 2013.

Didion, Joan. *We Tell Ourselves Stories in Order to Live: Collected Nonfiction*. New York: Alfred A. Knopf, 2006.

Dostoyevsky, Fyodor. *The Idiot*. New York: Modern Library, 1962.

Gardner, John. *The Art of Fiction: Notes on Craft for Young Writers*. New York: Vintage Books, 1991.

Gladiator. Directed by Ridley Scott. Performed by Russell Crowe and Joaquin Phoenix. DreamWorks L.L.C and Universal Studios, 2000.

Hale, Mike. "No Longer 'Lost' but Still Searching." *The New York Times* online, May 25, 2010. http://www.nytimes.com/2010/05/25/arts/television/25lost.html?

The Hobbit: An Unexpected Journey (film adaptation). Directed by Peter Jackson. Performed by Ian McKellen and Martin Freeman. New Line Cinema, 2012.

Hoffman, Claire. "Mr. and Mr. Smith: Will and Jaden Psych Up for After Earth." *Vulture*, May 26, 2013. http://www.vulture.com/2013/05/will-and-jaden-smith-on-working-together.html?mid=nymag_press.

The Hudsucker Proxy. Directed by Joel Coen and Ethan Coen. Performed by Tim Robbins, Paul Newman, and Jennifer Jason Leigh. Polygram Filmed Entertainment, 1994.

Hunter, James Davison. *To Change the World*. New York: Oxford University Press, 2010.

Hurwitz, Mitchell, writer. "Key Decisions." *Arrested Development*. Fox. November 23, 2003.

Indiana Jones and the Last Crusade. Directed by Steven Spielberg. Performed by Harrison Ford and Sean Connery. Paramount Pictures, 1989.

Inglourious Basterds. Directed by Quentin Tarantino. Performed by Brad Pitt and Eli Roth. Universal Pictures, 2009.

James, Etta, Harvey Fuqua, and Riley Hampton, writers. *At Last!* Chess/MCA, 1999, MP3.

Jerome. *The Homilies of Saint Jerome*. Vol. Z. The Fathers of the Church. Washington, DC: The Catholic University of America Press, 1966.

Johnson, Clark, writer. "The Target." *The Wire*. HBO. June 2, 2002.

"Jon Hamm: My Comments Regarding Kim Kardashian Were 'Taken Out of Context.'" *Access Hollywood* online, March 14, 2012. http://www.accesshollywood.com/jon-hamm-my-comments-regarding-kim-kardashian-were-taken-out-of-context_article_61948.

Jurassic Park. Directed by Steven Spielberg. Performed by Jeff Goldblum. Universal Pictures, 1993. DVD.

Kardashian, Kim. Twitter post. March 12, 2012, 3:20 p.m. https://twitter.com/KimKardashian/status/179285840244125696.

Keillor, Garrison. *Good Poems for Hard Times*. New York: Viking, 2005.

Kerouac, Jack. *On the Road*. New York: Penguin, 1955.

Works Cited

King, Stephen. *Dark Macabre*. New York: Gallery Books, 1981.

Lamar, Cyriaque. "Jeff Bridges and Olivia Wilde Say TRON Legacy Is All about Religion." *io9*, December 14, 2010. http://io9.com/5713435/jeff-bridges -and-olivia-wilde-tell-us-about-the-zen-of-tron-legacy.

Lane, Belden. *The Solace of Fierce Landscapes*. New York: Oxford University Press, 2007.

Lewis, C. S. *The Weight of Glory*. London: Society for Promoting Christian Knowledge, 1942.

Lipsky, David, and David Foster Wallace. *Although of Course You End Up Becoming Yourself: A Road Trip with David Foster Wallace*. New York: Broadway Books, 2010.

Manhattan. Directed by Woody Allen. By Woody Allen, Marshall Brickman, and Gordon Willis. Produced by Charles H. Joffe. Performed by Woody Allen, Diane Keaton, Michael Murphy, Mariel Hemingway, Meryl Streep, and Anne Byrne Kronenfeld. United Artists Corporation, 1979.

Manos, James, Jr., writer. "The Big One." *Dexter*. Showtime. December 12, 2010.

McGee, Ryan. "Here Comes Honey Boo Boo." *A.V. Club*, August 8, 2012. http://www.avclub.com/articles/here-comes-honey-boo-boo,83569/.

Melville, Herman. *Bartleby, the Scrivener*. Munich: Langenscheidt-Longman, 1986.

———. *Moby-Dick*. Pleasantville, NY: Reader's Digest Association, 1989.

Miller, Donald. *A Million Miles in a Thousand Years: What I Learned While Editing My Life*. Nashville, TN: Thomas Nelson, 2010.

Mitchell, Joni, writer. "Woodstock." *Ladies of the Canyon*. Luxury Multimedia, 2005, MP3.

Morrison, Grant. *Supergods: What Masked Vigilantes, Miraculous Mutants, and a Sun God from Smallville Can Teach Us about Being Human*. New York: Spiegel Grau, 2011.

Naughton, John. "Daniel Craig: A Very Secret Agent." *GQ British* online, December 21, 2011. http://www.gq-magazine.co.uk/entertainment/articles /2012-01/03/daniel-craig-interview/page/3.

Nielson Company. "State of the Media: Trends in TV Viewing—2011 TV Upfronts," 2011. http://www.nielsen.com/content/dam/corporate/us/en /newswire/uploads/2011/04/State-of-the-Media-2011-TV-Upfronts.pdf.

Overstreet, Jeffrey. "The Naked Truth." *Christianity Today* online, July 2001. http://www.christianitytoday.com/ct/2001/julyweb-only/7-16-42.0.html ?paging=off.

Proust, Marcel. *In Search of Lost Time*. vol. 6 *Finding Time Again*. New York: Penguin, 1927.

Pulp Fiction. Directed by Quentin Tarantino. Performed by Samuel L. Jackson and Uma Thurman. Miramax, 1994.

Rushdie, Salman. *Joseph Anton: A Memoir*. New York: Random House, 2012.

Santiago, Christina. "Facebook Redesigns: Music, Movies and More." *CBS News* online, Sept. 22, 2011. http://www.cbsnews.com/news/facebook -redesigns-music-movies-and-more/.

Serling, Rod, writer. *The Twilight Zone*. CBS.

Serpe, Gina. "Jon Hamm: Kim Kardashian Slam 'Not Personal'" *E!Online*, March 14, 2012. http://www.eonline.com/news/301003/jon-hamm-kim -kardashian-slam-not-personal.

Shelley, Mary Wollstonecraft. *Frankenstein*. New York: Dover Publications, 1994.

Shill, Steve, writer. "All Prologue." *The Wire*. HBO. July 6, 2003.

Silverman, Craig. *Regret the Error: How Media Mistakes Pollute the Press and Imperil Free Speech*. New York: Sterling, 2007.

Simon, David, writer. "Unto Others." *The Wire*. HBO. October 29, 2006.

Smith, James K. A. *Desiring the Kingdom: Worship, Worldview, and Cultural Formation*. Grand Rapids, MI: Baker, 2009.

———. *Imagining the Kingdom: How Worship Works*. Grand Rapids, MI: Baker, 2013.

Solomon, Rosalyn. "Kim Kardashian Talks Makeup and Business." *Toronto Sun* online, October 20, 2010. http://www.torontosun.com/life/fashion/2010 /10/19/15750746.html.

Sparks, Alannah. "Jon Hamm Versus Kim Kardashian." *ELLEUK.com*, March 14, 2012. http://www.elleuk.com/star-style/news/jon-hamm-versus-kim -kardashian.

Tolkien, J. R. R., and Alan Lee, illustrator. *The Return of the King*. Boston: Houghton Mifflin, 2002.

Turkle, Sherry. "The Flight from Conversation." *The New York Times* online, April 22, 2012. http://www.nytimes.com/2012/04/22/opinion/sunday/the -flight-from-conversation.html?pagewanted=all_r=0.

Twenge, Jean M., and W. Keith Campbell. *The Narcissism Epidemic: Living in the Age of Entitlement*. New York: Free Press, 2009.

Wallace, David Foster. *Infinite Jest*. New York: Back Bay Books, 1996.

———. *A Supposedly Fun Thing I'll Never Do Again: Essays and Arguments*. Reprint ed. New York: Back Bay Books, 1998.

Weiner, Matthew, writer. "The Better Half." *Mad Men*. AMC. May 26, 2013.

Works Cited

————. "Man with a Plan." *Mad Men*. AMC. May 12, 2013.

————. "Meditations in an Emergency." *Mad Men*. AMC. October 26, 2008.

————. "The New Girl." *Mad Men*. AMC. August 24, 2008.

————. "Nixon vs. Kennedy." *Mad Men*. AMC. October 11, 2007.

————. "Smoke Gets in Your Eyes." *Mad Men*. AMC. July 19, 2007.

————. "The Suitcase." *Mad Men*. AMC. May 5, 2010.

————. "The Wheel." *Mad Men*. AMC. October 18, 2007.

Wolf, Gary. "Steve Jobs: The Next Insanely Great Thing." *Wired* online, February 1996. http://www.wired.com/wired/archive/4.02/jobs_pr.html.

Wright, N. T. *The Original Jesus: The Life and Vision of a Revolutionary*. Grand Rapids, MI: Eerdmans, 1996.

————. *Surprised by Hope: Rethinking Heaven, the Resurrection, and the Mission of the Church*. New York: HarperOne, 2008.

Zuckerburg, Mark. "An Open Letter from Facebook Founder Mark Zuckerburg." *The Facebook Blog*, December 1, 2009. https://www.facebook.com/blog/blog.php?post=190423927130.

NOTES

Introduction: A World Full of Stories

1. Laser discs were precursors to DVDs—big, pizza-sized CDs with high quality uncompressed digital data, requiring flipping every forty-five minutes or so like a vinyl LP.
2. Unfortunately, this gem isn't available on DVD, but if you ask a teenager, he can probably find a copy streaming online for free.
3. Smith, *Imagining the Kingdom*, 32.
4. The United States no longer exists in David Foster Wallace's book, and is now called O.N.A.N.
5. Wallace, *Infinite Jest*, 106.
6. Lipsky and Wallace, *Although of Course You End Up Becoming Yourself*, 81.
7. Smith, *Desiring the Kingdom*, 54.
8. Ibid., 58.
9. Wallace, *A Supposedly Fun Thing I'll Never Do Again*, "E Unibus Pluram," 27.
10. Ibid., 39.
11. Ibid., 34.

Chapter 1: The Stories We Tell

1. Rushdie, *Joseph Anton: A Memoir*, 19.
2. Wright, *The Original Jesus*, 36.
3. Tolkien, *The Return of the King*, 930.

Chapter 2: How Far Is Too Far?

1. Wolf, "Steve Jobs: The Next Insanely Great Thing."
2. Landis, *Coming to America*.
3. The issue of nudity in art in general and in film in particular has been a source of conflict and debate for some time. There's no doubt that Hollywood takes advantage of the human form to scandalize and tantalize, but is there ever a place for nudity? For some, it's a black-and-white issue. For others it's a matter of context.

    A few years ago, *Christianity Today* published "The Naked Truth," which contained a diversity of perspectives on when and if nudity is ever appropriate (Overstreet, "The Naked Truth"). This article may be a good starting place for wrestling with the issue.

It may also be valuable to consider the ways we view movies and TV shows that may contain sexually charged content. In our day of video on-demand, DVRs, and DVDs, we are rarely forced to sit through a scene that tantalizes or disturbs. Technology affords us many ways to fast-forward.

4. Cosper, "The 3 Most Disturbing Words on TV."
5. Melville, *Moby-Dick*, 147.
6. Nielson Company, "State of the Media: Trends in TV Viewing—2011 TV Upfronts."
7. Wallace, *A Supposedly Fun Thing I'll Never Do Again*, 53.

Chapter 3: The Ghosts of Eden

1. Proust, *In Search of Lost Time*, 179.
2. Abrams, Lieber, and Lindelof, "Through the Looking Glass," *Lost*.
3. Berry, "The Wild Birds," in *That Distant Land*, 356.
4. Payne, *The Descendants*.
5. Keillor, *Good Poems for Hard Times*, XVI.
6. Mitchell, "Woodstock," *Ladies of the Canyon*.
7. Quoted in Silverman, *Regret the Error*, 168.
8. My friend (and one of this book's editors) Collin Hansen pointed out dynamite's legacy in Birmingham. Dynamite contributed to the build-up of the city, but it also was used in the horrendous church bombing in 1963 that killed four little girls.
9. Shelley, *Frankenstein*, 53.
10. Ibid.
11. Spielberg, *Jurassic Park*.
12. Ibid.
13. "Jeff Bridges and Olivia Wilde Say TRON Legacy Is All about Religion," *io9*.
14. Morrison, *Supergods*, xiv.

Chapter 4: The Search for Love

1. James, *At Last!*
2. Hurwitz, "Key Decisions," *Arrested Development*.
3. Dostoyevsky, *The Idiot*, 367.
4. Allen, *Manhattan*.
5. Scott, *Gladiator*.
6. Didion, *We Tell Ourselves Stories in Order to Live*.

Chapter 5: O, How the Mighty Have Fallen

1. Lane, *The Solace of Fierce Landscapes*, 55–56.
2. Augustine, *The Confessions of St. Augustine*, 103.
3. Ibid., 1.

4. Weiner, "Smoke Gets in Your Eyes," *Mad Men*.
5. Ibid.
6. Ibid.
7. David and Seinfeld, "The Finale," *Seinfeld*.
8. Weiner, "The Wheel," *Mad Men*.
9. Weiner, "The New Girl," *Mad Men*.
10. Weiner, "Meditations in an Emergency," *Mad Men*.
11. Weiner, "Man with a Plan," *Mad Men*.
12. Weiner, "The Better Half," *Mad Men*.
13. Weiner, "The Suitcase," *Mad Men*.
14. Weiner, "Nixon vs. Kennedy," *Mad Men*.
15. Ibid.

Chapter 6: Frustration
1. Spielberg, *Indiana Jones and the Last Crusade*.
2. Melville, *Bartleby, the Scrivener*, 14.
3. Johnson, "The Target," *The Wire*.
4. Haggis, *Crash*.
5. Shill, "All Prologue," *The Wire*.
6. Simon, "Unto Others," *The Wire*.
7. Shill, "All Prologue," *The Wire*.

Chapter 7: Shadows and Darkness
1. King, *Dark Macabre*, 13.
2. Serling, *The Twilight Zone*.
3. Ibid.
4. Carter, "Jose Chung's 'From Outer Space,'" *The X-Files*.
5. Carter, "Clyde Bruckman's Final Response," *The X-Files*.
6. Ibid.
7. Ibid.
8. Hale, "No Longer 'Lost' But Still Searching."

Chapter 8: Redemptive Violence
1. Coen and Coen, *The Hudsucker Proxy*.
2. Manos, "The Big One," *Dexter*.
3. Ibid.
4. Ibid.
5. Ibid.
6. Ibid.
7. Ibid.
8. Tarantino, *Pulp Fiction*.
9. Ibid.
10. Ibid.

11. Ibid.
12. Ibid.
13. Tarantino, *Inglourious Basterds*.

Chapter 9: Heroes and Messiahs
  1. Jerome, *The Homilies of Saint Jerome*, n.p.
  2. Wright, *Surprised by Hope*, 246.
  3. Jackson, film adaptation of *The Hobbit: An Unexpected Journey*.
  4. Coen and Coen, *The Big Lebowski*.
  5. Morrison, *Supergods*, 15.
  6. Detweiler, *Man of Steel*, 6.

Chapter 10: Honey Boo Boo and the Weight of Glory
  1. Twenge and Campbell, *The Narcissism Epidemic*, 91.
  2. Brockes, "Kim Kardashian: My Life as a Brand," *The Guardian* online.
  3. Hoffman, "Mr. and Mr. Smith: Will and Jaden Psych Up for After Earth," *Vulture*.
  4. Naughton, "Daniel Craig: A Very Secret Agent," *British GQ* online.
  5. Sparks, "Jon Hamm Versus Kim Kardashian," *ELLEUK*.com
  6. Kardashian, Twitter post, March 12, 2012, 3:20 p.m. https://twitter.com /KimKardashian/status/179285840244125696
  7. Serpe, "Jon Hamm: Kim Kardashian Slam 'Not Personal,'" *E!Online*.
  8. "Jon Hamm: My Comments Regarding Kim Kardashian Were 'Taken Out of Context,'" *Access Hollywood* online.
  9. McGee, "Here Comes Honey Boo Boo," *A.V. Club*.
  10. Solomon, "Kim Kardashian Talks Makeup and Business," *Toronto Sun* online.
  11. Miller, *A Million Miles in a Thousand Years*, 20.
  12. Zuckerburg, "An Open Letter from Facebook Founder Mark Zuckerberg," *The Facebook Blog*.
  13. Christina Santiago, "Facebook Redesigns: Music, Movies and More."
  14. Turkle, "The Flight from Conversation," *The New York Times* online.
  15. Lewis, *Weight of Glory*, 26.
  16. Ibid., 36.
  17. Ibid., 37.
  18. Gardner, *The Art of Fiction*, 32.
  19. Lewis, *Weight of Glory*, 41.

Epilogue (And a Word to Christian Filmmakers)
  1. Smith, *Desiring the Kingdom*, 109–10.
  2. Lewis, *Weight of Glory*, 15.
  3. Kerouac, *On the Road*, 5.
  4. Hunter, *To Change the World*, 41–43.

GENERAL INDEX

General Index

SCRIPTURE INDEX

Scripture Index

Also Available from Mike Cosper